Proving the Catholic Faith Is Biblical

Other books by Dave Armstrong
from Sophia Institute Press:

The Catholic Verses
A Biblical Defense of Catholicism
The Quotable Newman
Bible Proofs for Catholic Truths
The One-Minute Apologist

Dave Armstrong

Proving the Catholic Faith Is Biblical

From Priestly Celibacy to the Rosary:
80 Short Essays Explaining the
Biblical Basis of Catholicism

SOPHIA INSTITUTE PRESS
Manchester, New Hampshire

Copyright © 2015 by Dave Armstrong
Printed in the United States of America. All rights reserved.

Cover design: Coronation Media in collaboration with Perceptions Design Studio.

On the cover: "Books on wooden table" (144613493) © donatas1205/Shutterstock.com and "Grunge texture" (136495241) © Allgusak/Shutterstock.com

Chapters 1, 8, 30-31, 51-52, and 80 of this book were originally published in *The Michigan Catholic* (May to August 2014). Chapters 9, 25-27, 32-34, 39-40, 42-43, 45, 61-62, 77, and 78 were originally published in *Seton Magazine* (March to July 2014).

Biblical citations are from the Revised Standard Version of the Bible (© 1971) copyrighted by the Division of Christian Education of the National Council of the Churches of Christ in the United States of America. All emphases have been added.

No part of this book may be reproduced, stored in a retrieval system, or transmitted in any form, or by any means, electronic, mechanical, photocopying, or otherwise, without the prior written permission of the publisher, except by a reviewer, who may quote brief passages in a review.

Sophia Institute Press
Box 5284, Manchester, NH 03108
1-800-888-9344
www.SophiaInstitute.com

Sophia Institute Press® is a registered trademark of Sophia Institute.

Library of Congress Cataloging-in-Publication Data
Armstrong, Dave, 1958-
 [Essays. Selections]
 Proving the Catholic faith Is biblical: from priestly celibacy to the rosary: 80 short Essays explaining the biblical basis of Catholicism / Dave Armstrong.
   pages cm
 Includes bibliographical references and index.
 ISBN 978-1-62282-263-8 (pbk. : alk. paper) 1. Catholic Church—Apologetic works. 2. Catholic Church—Doctrines. 3. Bible—Criticism, interpretation, etc. I. Title.
 BX1752.A767 2015
 282—dc23
                                                                    2015013817

First printing

*To my beautiful wife, Judy,
without whom my career, as it has proceeded,
would have been impossible.
I'm deeply grateful always
for your never-ending support.*

Contents

Introduction xiii
1. Tradition Is Not Always a Bad Word in Scripture 3
2. The "Three-Legged Stool" vs. *Sola Scriptura* 8
3. Centuries of Wisdom from the Church 11
4. How to Search the Scriptures 14
5. Ten Examples of How the New Testament
   Reflects the Old Testament 17
6. Why We Accept the Catholic Church's Claims 20
7. Catholic Ecclesiology and the Jerusalem Council . . . 22
8. Three Biblical Arguments
   for the Authority of the Church 24
9. Calling Catholic Priests *Father* 28
10. We Believe *All That* the
    Catholic Church Teaches 32
11. The Claim to Be the One True Church 37

12. On Whether God Would Protect
    His Church from Error 40
13. Are Church Councils
    More Authoritative Than Popes? 43
14. Catholic Priestly Celibacy 47
15. The Celibate Priesthood as a Higher Calling 49
16. A New Argument for Mandatory Priestly Celibacy? . . 53
17. Works Can Be Good or Bad, Just Like Traditions . . . 57
18. Faith and Works 59
19. Belief in Jesus Requires Obedience to Him 64
20. Faith Calls for Confidence and Perseverance 67
21. The "Unanswered" Prayers of Jesus 69
22. St. John vs. John Calvin on Limited Atonement 74
23. God Does Not Predestine the Damned 77
24. Prayer, Penance, and the Eternal Destiny of Others . . 79
25. Biblical Support for Lent 83
26. Divine Chastisement (or, Purgatory in *This* Life) 87
27. Mystery Is No Basis for
    Rejecting Transubstantiation 90
28. On the Nature of Idolatry 94
29. "The Apostle Paul Says He Is a Priest? Where?" 97
30. Sacramentalism 99

31. Ritualistic and Formal Worship 103
32. Is the Rosary "Vain Repetition"? 107
33. Asking Saints to Intercede Is a Teaching of Jesus 110
34. Praying to Angels and Angelic Intercession 113
35. Worshipping God through Images in Scripture 117
36. Martin Luther and the Intercession of the Saints 119
37. The False Doctrine of "Soul Sleep" 122
38. Veneration of Saints 126
39. The Perpetual Virginity of Mary 128
40. Mary's Consecrated Virginity 134
41. A Rationalist Objection to the Virgin Birth 138
42. Martin Luther and the
    Immaculate Purification of Mary 141
43. Mary's Immaculate Conception 145
44. Mary Is the Mother of God 149
45. The Assumption of the Blessed Virgin Mary 151
46. Mary the Queen Mother and Queen of Heaven 155
47. The Virgin Mary in the Book of Revelation 157
48. Biblical Analogies for Marian Apparitions 160
49. Protestant Difficulties
    Regarding Papal Infallibility 166

50. Why It Is Easy to Know
    What Catholics Should Believe 170

51. The Bible Never Says That Jesus Is God? Wrong! . . .174

52. The Holy Trinity Proven from Scripture 178

53. Is Trinitarianism Demonstrable
    from Scripture Alone? 182

54. Trinitarian Baptismal Formula
    and "Jesus Only" Baptism 185

55. Should God the Father Be
    Visually Depicted in Paintings? 190

56. Satan's Tempting of Jesus
    as a Proof of Jesus' Divinity. 192

57. Jesus' Acceptance of Praise
    as a Proof of His Divinity. 194

58. Jesus Is Explicitly, Directly
    Called "God" (Romans 9:5) 196

59. Jesus' Agony in the Garden vs. "Be Not Anxious" . . .198

60. Annulment Is Not Catholic Divorce 201

61. "Be Fruitful and Multiply" 205

62. God Blesses Parents with Children 208

63. Onan's Sin and Punishment 212

64. Reply to an Attack against
    NFP and Spacing of Children 216

65. Contraception, Murder, and the Contralife Will 220
66. Does the Bible Condemn Homosexual Acts? 226
67. St. Paul's Argument from Nature
    against Homosexual Acts 230
68. The Prohibition against Premarital Sex 234
69. Does 1 Corinthians Sanction Premarital Sex? 239
70. Thoughts on Women's Ordination 244
71. Philosophical Defense of the Necessity of Hell 247
72. The Stupidity of the Devil 254
73. Demonic Possession or Epilespy? 257
74. The Reality of Hell .260
75. A Perfect God Creating an Imperfect World 266
76. Can God Be Blamed for the Nazi Holocaust? 268
77. The Inevitability of Development of Doctrine 273
78. New Testament Proofs of Noah's Existence 277
79. Jesus' Use of Socratic Method 280
80. Apologetics Isn't Saying
    You're Sorry for Your Faith! 285

    About the Author: Dave Armstrong 289

xi

Introduction

This is a collection of essays that are (1) short (usually two or three pages), (2) characterized by lots of biblical argumentation, and (3) written in defense of Catholicism (apologetics). Most of them came about as a result of my ongoing efforts to comment on issues that regularly come up in "worlds" of Catholic apologetics and theology online.

The brevity of the chapters indicates the trend in my apologetic writing for many years now: "quick," precise answers to apologetics questions. For better or ill, this is the world that we live in, and the apologist must make efforts (as St. Paul did, and as Vatican II stressed) to meet people where they are.

I don't deny the continuing utility and necessity of longer treatments (my "corpus" still contains plenty of those!), but most people prefer shorter essays, and their interest in theology and apologetics generally doesn't extend to treatise-length expositions. This is all the truer for beginners in theology.

Many of these essays were written as columns for *Seton Magazine*, which is devoted to Catholic homeschoolers. Others came from my regular column in *The Michigan Catholic*, the official newspaper for the Archdiocese of Detroit. Some were originally posted as part of my work in the Internet forum of the Coming

Proving the Catholic Faith Is Biblical

Home Network from 2007 to 2010 (I was the head moderator during that period), and several were initiated on Facebook. All of these essays are meant to answer the questions that people ask and to make the Catholic Faith more understandable, leading to a confident belief and the ability to "make a defense" (1 Pet. 3:15) for this Faith as opportunities arise. I hope by God's grace I have accomplished these goals.

Thanks so much for reading, and God bless you!

Proving the Catholic Faith Is Biblical

1

Tradition Is Not Always a Bad Word in Scripture

One might loosely define tradition as the authoritative and authentic Christian history of theological doctrines and devotional practices. Christianity is fundamentally grounded in the earth-shattering historical events in the life of Jesus Christ (His Incarnation, preaching, miracles, Passion, Crucifixion, Resurrection, and Ascension).

Eyewitnesses (Luke 1:1-2; Acts 1:1-3; 2 Pet. 1:16-18) communicated these true stories to the early Christians, who in turn passed them on to other Christians (under the guidance of the Church's authority) down through the ages. Therefore, Christian tradition, defined as authentic Church history, is unavoidable, and is a very *good* thing: not a bad thing at all.

Many read the accounts of Jesus' conflicts with the Pharisees and get the idea that He was utterly opposed to all tradition whatsoever. This is not true. A close reading of passages such as Matthew 15:3-9 and Mark 7:8-13 will reveal that He condemned only *corrupt* traditions of men, not tradition per se.

Jesus uses qualifying phrases such as "*your* tradition," "precepts *of men*," "tradition *of men*," as opposed to "word of God" or

Proving the Catholic Faith Is Biblical

"the commandment of God" and so forth. St. Paul makes exactly the same contrast:

> **Colossians 2:8**: See to it that no one makes a prey of you by philosophy and empty deceit, according to *human* tradition, according to the elemental spirits of the universe, and not according to *Christ*.

The New Testament explicitly teaches that traditions can be either good (from God) or bad (from men, when against God's true traditions). Corrupt traditions from the Pharisees were *bad*, although many of their *legitimate* teachings were recognized by Jesus (see, e.g., Matt. 23:3). The spoken gospel and the apostolic writings (some eventually formulated as Holy Scripture) were altogether good: the authentic Christian tradition as revealed by the incarnate God to the apostles and "ratified" by the Church.

The Greek word for *tradition* in the New Testament is *paradosis*. It occurs in Colossians 2:8 and in the following three passages (among others):

> **1 Corinthians 11:2**: [M]aintain the traditions even as I have delivered them to you.

> **2 Thessalonians 2:15**: [S]tand firm and hold to the traditions which you were taught by us, either by word of mouth or by letter.

> **2 Thessalonians 3:6**: the tradition that you received from us.

St. Paul makes no distinction between written and oral tradition. He doesn't regard oral Christian tradition as bad and undesirable. This is made even clearer in two other statements to Timothy:

> **2 Timothy 1:13**: Follow the pattern of the sound words which you have heard from me.
>
> **2 Timothy 2:2**: and what you have heard from me before many witnesses entrust to faithful men who will be able to teach others also.

St. Paul is here urging Timothy not only to "follow" the oral teaching that Timothy had "heard from" him but also to pass it on to *others*. This is a clear picture of authentic historical continuity of Christian doctrine—precisely what the Catholic Church calls *sacred tradition* or, when emphasizing the teaching authority of bishops in the Church, *apostolic succession*.

The phrase "deposit of faith" is also used to describe the original gospel teaching as handed over or delivered to the apostles (see, e.g., Acts 2:42; Jude 3). The Catholic Church considers herself merely the "custodian" or "guardian" of this public revelation or "deposit" from God, because we believe that God set up His Church (Matthew 16), making St. Peter the leader, and that the Church has continued through history ever since. It's all God's doing, not ours. We participate in His plan only by His grace and mercy.

When the first Christians went out and preached the gospel of Jesus Christ after Pentecost, this was oral tradition. Some of it was recorded in the Bible (e.g., in Acts 2) but most was not, and indeed could not be, for sheer volume (see John 20:30; 21:25). It was primarily this oral Christian tradition, not the text of the New Testament (many, if not most, people couldn't read then anyway) that turned the world upside down).

Proving the Catholic Faith Is Biblical

Accordingly, when the phrases "word of God" or "word of the Lord" occur in Acts and in the epistles, they almost always refer to oral preaching, not to the written word of the Bible, as many Protestants (and probably a lot of Catholics, too) casually assume.

The New Testament itself is a record of primitive, apostolic Christianity. It is a development, so to speak, of both the Old Testament and early oral Christian preaching, teaching, and tradition. The process of canonization of the New Testament took more than three hundred years and involved taking into account human opinions and traditions as to which books were believed to be Scripture. It was not immediately obvious to all Christians (as some foolishly assume or argue).

Many notable Church Fathers accepted books as part of Scripture that are not now so recognized (e.g., *The Shepherd of Hermas*, the *Didache*, the epistle of Barnabas, 1 Clement). Many others didn't accept certain canonical books until very late (e.g., Hebrews, James, 2 Peter, and Revelation). Thus, the Bible cannot be separated and isolated from tradition and a developmental process.

In Catholicism, Scripture and tradition are intrinsically interwoven. They have been described as "twin fonts of the one divine wellspring" (revelation), and cannot be separated, any more than can two wings of a bird, two sides of a coin, or two blades of a pair of scissors.

The Church also has strong authority, so that the Catholic rule of faith consists of Scripture, tradition, and the Church. This may be imagined as a three-legged stool. If you remove any one of the legs, the stool collapses; all three are equally necessary for it to stand up.

Tradition Is Not Always a Bad Word in Scripture

That is Catholicism: and (if anyone wonders about it) all these notions are firmly backed up by *Scripture itself*, without any contradiction as regards Catholic tradition or Church dogma and doctrine.

2

The "Three-Legged Stool" vs. *Sola Scriptura*

Catholics believe in faith that sacred Scripture, sacred tradition, and the authority of the Catholic Church do not and *will not* conflict. They are viewed as pieces of a whole, just as Protestants believe (in faith) that Scripture doesn't contradict itself and is a harmonious, coherent whole, all the while devoting whole books to supposed Bible difficulties that present a challenge to many readers and believers. One can believe in faith that an answer to a "difficulty" exists and at the same time not deny that there is (on the surface, anyway) a seeming difficulty that requires much scholarship and study to resolve.

Sacred Scripture is true, and God's inspired, infallible, written Word and revelation. Catholics have always believed this. The scholar Harold Lindsell, former editor of *Christianity Today*, in his book *Battle for the Bible*, joyfully acknowledged that fact and then demonstrated how many Protestant denominations have eroded or denied this doctrine of faith.

The Bible is central and primary in Catholicism as well, but not *exclusively authoritative*. It's not isolated, or by itself, nor can it even logically be so. We maintain that this was the apostolic and patristic viewpoint, and that of St. Augustine and St. Thomas Aquinas, which we preserve unchanged.

The "Three-Legged Stool" vs. *Sola Scriptura*

The Bible itself points to tradition and the Church as authoritative (for example, the Jerusalem Council in Acts 15); it doesn't teach that it alone is the Christian's sole ultimate authority, and, of course, it was the Church that declared the parameters of what books were Scripture in the first place. The famous Presbyterian author R. C. Sproul has noted that the canon was "a fallible collection of infallible books."

Scripture is what it is, in its essence, and always has been, yet the Church was necessary to settle a matter (the canon) that had indeed achieved a general or broad consensus, yet not without many deviations from what we now regard as Scripture. Some Church fathers thought 1 and 2 Clement and the epistle of Barnabas were Scripture, and books such as Revelation and James were very late in being generally received as such.

So we believe through faith and reason and Scripture that God will protect the Church from error in her dogmatic pronouncements, because we believe there is one institutional Church (and "one faith," as St. Paul states), handed down (again, according to Paul) from the apostles, with which other Christians can implicitly be connected, to a greater or lesser degree (particularly by baptism and common beliefs, such as the tenets of the Nicene Creed).

Protestants believe that God protected Holy Scripture from error, by means of inspiration, even though sinful, fallible men wrote it. Catholics agree with that and also believe that God (the Holy Spirit: John 14-16) can protect His Church from error (a merely "negative" and preventive guarantee), by means of infallibility (a lesser supernatural gift than inspiration), even though sinful, fallible men are involved in it.

If God can do one thing, He can do the other. Since we see these things indicated in Scripture and apostolic tradition, we

Proving the Catholic Faith Is Biblical

believe them. It takes much faith, because now we are dealing with a human (yet divinely guided) institution, yet this faith is not without biblical and reasonable grounds.

The Catholic Church authoritatively interprets the Bible. But Protestants *also* interpret (and *have* to interpret) the Bible, just as we do. The Bible isn't self-evident. And this is why Protestants notoriously disagree on many major issues. The real choice, then, isn't Bible versus Church but rather an individual or denominational interpretation of the Bible versus an interpretation of an authoritative Church based on two thousand years of unbroken developing biblical, apostolic, and patristic tradition and theology.

Seen that way, the Catholic approach is, I submit, more plausible because it has historical substance and continuity and isn't individualistic or sectarian, nor does it fall into an unbiblical, either-or type of thinking.

3

Centuries of Wisdom from the Church

The Protestant (especially evangelicals and charismatics — I have been in both camps) tends to look at Scripture and say, "What does this teach *me*?" As far as that goes, there is nothing wrong with it, except when all these individuals look at the same Scripture, which they all revere as the inspired, infallible Word of God, and disagree on the *interpretation*. Then we have a problem, because contradiction means someone is wrong, and wrong is a falsehood, and falsehood comes from the devil, the father of lies. Truth is not relative.

The Catholic Church (contrary to the false stereotype) accepts and encourages the individual to read the Bible, but goes *much* further and deeper than that. G. K. Chesterton said that tradition was the "democracy of the dead." What he was getting at was the *communal* aspect of historical Christianity. The Catholic believes that the Church has learned a few things over the years and that these can be passed on so that we don't have to reinvent the wheel in every generation.

The Catholic asks not only what God is communicating to him *individually* but also what He has taught all the millions of *other* Christians throughout history: holy people, saints, Doctors, missionaries, priests, nuns, fervent laypeople. That's the whole thing about the Church Fathers. They were the "on fire" Christians of the early centuries. What did they believe? What can we learn from them?

We choose the "democracy of the dead" rather than a head count of those of us who happen to be here today or some vote at a national convention or a poll in *Christianity Today*. We believe that if God teaches us things personally, He also teaches other folks too and has done so all along, so that we can learn from them. To a large extent, this is what tradition is. It's really no more complicated than that.

Protestants have run down and disparaged tradition as barnacles on a ship, to be scraped off, or as corruption, for so long that they miss the simple, obvious beauty of the thing: the democracy of the dead—the community of the saints, gathered not just geographically (like the Jerusalem Council of Acts 15) but over time as well, throughout history.

Whatever we can ponder in our heads, the Church has, inevitably, thought about for centuries, and has come to conclusions. Catholics trust these, as a function of trust in God, who guides and protects His Church, as we believe. It doesn't mean that the Church has always been perfect in every way, about everything, but when something has been "officially" declared by pope, council, or official catechism, we can accept it as trustworthy.

The individual doesn't have to figure everything out. That's impractical and, I contend, impossible anyway. Who of us is the font of all wisdom? How silly is *that* notion! Who even wants to *have* that burden and responsibility? God never meant His Church or the individual Christian to function that way. There is something far greater than merely our own private judgment and discernment.

Centuries of Wisdom from the Church

That is Catholicism. What has been believed in the past and passed down is extremely important. The Church eventually develops these thoughts and proclaims dogmas, after (usually) many centuries of reflection.

4

How to Search the Scriptures

St. Paul's authority was accepted in faith by his followers. He spoke with great authority. He said he was delivering truth and tradition, and he expected his followers to accept it without question. There is no hint that he thought otherwise. No one denies that he had profound apostolic authority. The question is whether Scripture alone was the only infallible authority.

St. Paul *explained* things, and argued and defended and so forth, but his authority was unquestioned. So was the authority of the Church, which is why it held a council in Jerusalem and then Paul went out proclaiming the infallible (Acts 15:22, 28) decisions of the council (Acts 16:4) in his missionary journeys.

> **Acts 17:10-11**: The brethren immediately sent Paul and Silas away by night to Beroea; and when they arrived they went into the Jewish synagogue. Now these Jews were more noble than those in Thessalonica, for they received the word with all eagerness, examining the scriptures daily to see if these things were so.

The example of the Bereans does not disprove Catholic authority or suggest *sola Scriptura* at all. The word that they received with "all eagerness" was Paul's oral teaching and preaching, which

How to Search the Scriptures

they confirmed as consistent with Holy Scripture (as Catholics believe all legitimate tradition to be), and an additional revelation. Once they had done that, for them, his teaching was on a par with Scripture and of binding authority.

Searching the Scripture to confirm or defend some doctrine is not the same as *sola Scriptura*. The latter means making the Bible the *only* infallible authority. The mainstream tradition of the Jews at that time (in all likelihood including the Bereans) was Pharisaism, and it accepted oral tradition and an oral Torah received by Moses on Mt. Sinai, in addition to the written Torah. This in and of itself is fundamentally hostile to *sola Scriptura*. The ones who held to a strict Bible-alone view were the Sadducees, who accepted only the Torah (the first five books of the Bible). But they denied the resurrection of the righteous in the afterlife.

Searching the Scriptures in and of itself is not somehow opposed to Catholic authority (I do it all the time myself — and throughout this book — in order to defend and "confirm" Catholic teaching). When Jesus explained to the two disciples on the road to Emmaus the doctrine of the suffering Messiah (after His Resurrection), He did so by means of Scripture (Luke 24:25-27).

He authoritatively "interpreted to them in all the scriptures the things concerning himself" (Luke 24:27). This is the role of Church and Tradition. Scripture has to be interpreted by someone with authority. Our Lord did the same when He appeared to the eleven disciples (Luke 24:36-38). "Then he opened their minds to understand the scriptures" (Luke 24:45).

The Holy Spirit and the intervention of Jesus were required in order for them to understand. If we interpret on our own apart from the Holy Spirit and disregard for the apostolic tradition preserved by the Church, we can often be led astray (Acts 8:27-35; 2 Pet. 1:20-21; 3:16).

Proving the Catholic Faith Is Biblical

When certain Jews were opposing Jesus, He took them to task for searching the Scriptures (almost as an end in itself) but not seeing that the same Scripture testified to *Him* (John 5:39). In other words, they were trying to separate God from His Word, as if God's Word didn't direct men toward God Himself. St. Paul used the same method when he went to the Jews and proclaimed the gospel (see, e.g., Acts 17:2).

Now, if both Jesus and Paul argued from the Scriptures, then Jews who were considering whether their claims were true would naturally do the same. So the Bereans did exactly that. It was a both-and methodology. They weren't opposing one thing to the other. Both were true, and their harmony with each other confirmed that. They didn't rule out the possibility that the oral proclamation was true (simply because it was oral); they merely confirmed it from existing written, inspired revelation.

If they had been operating with an either-or mentality, on the other hand, they wouldn't have "received the [oral] word with all eagerness." They would have been highly skeptical of it and would have checked it against Scripture; and even if it lined up with Scripture, they would have denied that it was infallible unless it eventually made it into Scripture. But exactly what Paul said to them is *not* recorded in Scripture.

Catholics say that Paul's word was authoritative and infallible, whether it was "inscripturated" or not. But many Protestants argue (based on the false premise of *sola Scriptura*) that it only is if it is later recorded in Scripture (a distinction that is itself unbiblical, since Paul's words are presented as authoritative, *when they are spoken*).

5

Ten Examples of How the New Testament Reflects the Old Testament

1. **Matthew 6:7**: And in praying do not heap up empty phrases as the Gentiles do.

   Sirach 7:14: Do not prattle in the assembly of the elders, nor repeat yourself in your prayer.

2. **Matthew 6:12**: And forgive us our debts/As we also have forgiven our debtors

   Sirach 28:2: Forgive your neighbor the wrong he has done, and then your sins will be pardoned when you pray.

3. **Matthew 7:12**: So whatever you wish that men would do to you, do so to them; for this is the law and the prophets.

   Tobit 4:15: And what you hate, do not do to anyone.

4. **Matthew 7:16**: You will know them by their fruits.

   Sirach 27:6: The fruit discloses the cultivation of a tree.

5. **Luke 1:52**: [H]e has put down the mighty from their thrones, and exalted those of low degree.

   Sirach 10:14: The Lord has cast down the thrones of rulers, and has seated the lowly in their place.

6. **Acts 17:29**: Being then God's offspring, we ought not to think that the Deity is like gold, or silver, or stone, a representation by the art and imagination of man.

   Wisdom 13:10: But miserable, with their hopes set on dead things, are the men who give the name "gods" to the works of men's hands, gold and silver fashioned with skill, and likenesses of animals, or a useless stone, the work of an ancient hand.

7. **Romans 1:20**: Ever since the creation of the world his invisible nature, namely, his eternal power and deity, has been clearly perceived in the things that have been made.

   Wisdom 13:1: For all men who were ignorant of God were foolish by nature; and they were unable from the good things that are seen to know him who exists, nor did they recognize the craftsman while paying heed to his works.

8. **Romans 9:21**: Has the potter no right over the clay, to make out of the same lump one vessel for beauty and another for menial use?

   Wisdom 15:7: For when a potter kneads the soft earth and laboriously molds each vessel for our service, he fashions out of the same clay both the vessels that serve clean uses and those for contrary uses, making all in like manner; but which shall be the use of each of these the worker in clay decides.

9. **Hebrews 11:35**: Women received their dead by resurrection. Some were tortured, refusing to accept release, that they might rise again to a better life.

   2 Maccabees 7:28-29: I beseech you, my child, ... Do not fear this butcher, but prove worthy of your brothers. Accept death, so that in God's mercy I may get you back again with your brothers.

10. **Revelation 8:2**: Then I saw the seven angels who stand before God, and seven trumpets were given to them.

    Tobit 12:15: I am Raphael, one of the seven holy angels who present the prayers of the saints and enter into the presence of the glory of the Holy One.

6

Why We Accept the Catholic Church's Claims

The bottom line is that faith is a gift of God, by His grace. The very faith to believe that God not only made a way for salvation, but also provided an authoritative *Church*, through which He chose to channel that salvation and to provide guidance, is a *gift*. It doesn't come from our reasoning efforts. Reason can bring us up to the gates, but it can't prove that the gates and what lie behind them are what they *are*, or compel us to walk through them and enter in.

What reason and facts and evidence *can* do is to confirm over and over that the Catholic Church is right. When that happens so many times, it becomes easier (by the weight of cumulative evidence) to accept in faith that she is *always* right when she claims something dogmatically or infallibly. We must accept that there are things that we don't and can't understand and must believe because of what we *do* understand. No one can ever figure out every jot and tittle. For one thing, no one has the *time* to do so.

It's a matter of agreeing with biblical revelation that there is indeed such a thing as an authoritative Church, set up by God (and initiated by Jesus' commission to St. Peter in Matthew 16)

Why We Accept the Catholic Church's Claims

and then judging (again, led by grace and the Holy Spirit, the Helper) whether the Catholic claims are feasible and plausible.

My greatest struggle was with the notion of infallibility, so I understand that objection inside and out. But I kept studying and talking to Catholic friends and saw that none of the alternatives were plausible, and so I yielded myself.

I've become more and more assured of this truth during my nearly twenty-four years of defending it. The more I learn, the more my faith is strengthened (*never* weakened), and this is one of the joys of apologetics.

7

Catholic Ecclesiology and the Jerusalem Council

In the Catholic model, ecumenical councils make decisions (led and guided by the Holy Spirit) in tandem with the popes, who preside and have "veto power." It's both-and.

The Jerusalem Council (Acts 15) spoke for and to the entire Church. St. Paul then proclaimed its edicts in other regions — in this case, Asia Minor, or modern-day Turkey, which was quite a ways away — as binding and obligatory upon all:

> **Acts 15:25, 30**: [I]t has seemed good to us, having come to one accord, to choose men and send them to you with our beloved Barnabas and Paul.... So when they were sent off, they went down to Antioch; and having gathered the congregation together, they delivered the letter.
>
> **Acts 16:4**: As they went on their way through the cities, they delivered to them for observance the decisions which had been reached by the apostles and elders who were at Jerusalem.

If someone wants to argue that James presided at the council, he was still, nevertheless, acting as a bishop (of Jerusalem)

Catholic Ecclesiology and the Jerusalem Council

and presiding over a council that made binding legal decisions obligatory on all Christians everywhere. That's not congregationalism; it's not even Presbyterian government. It's clearly Episcopal/Catholic ecclesiology and contradicts some notion of local congregationalism or independent autonomy.

Some argue that it was merely a local council of Jerusalem (the great evangelical scholar F. F. Bruce takes that view). If so, how is it that Paul acts as he does in Asia Minor (Acts 16:4)? How can the Jerusalem Church have jurisdiction over those Christians unless episcopalian government is in place?

Moreover, the biblical text informs us that a letter was written to "the brethren who are of the Gentiles in Antioch and Syria and Cilicia" (Acts 15:23). It is written in the language of command (although gently so):

> **Acts 15:28-29**: For it has seemed good to the Holy Spirit and to us to lay upon you no greater burden than these necessary things: that you abstain from what has been sacrificed to idols and from blood and from what is strangled and from unchastity. If you keep yourselves from these, you will do well. Farewell.

How is it that one local church in Jerusalem (according to the nonepiscopal view) can give "binding orders" to other local churches far away? That is nonsensical in a congregational interpretation. But it makes perfect sense with an episcopal or even papal/Catholic view.

If this shows (as I think it does) a "higher" church authority giving binding decisions to Christians over wide geographical areas, then it is a model, by common sense. Otherwise, why is it included in revelation? These things are in Scripture for our instruction.

8

Three Biblical Arguments for the Authority of the Church

My friend Al Kresta (a Catholic radio talk-show host and author) once noted that in C. S. Lewis's famous book *Mere Christianity*, which was an ecumenical effort to find things that all Christians shared in common, and the "nonnegotiables" of Christianity, a central, crucial doctrine of two of the three major divisions of Christianity was omitted.

The great Anglican apologist did not include a doctrine of the Church as a binding authority in the Christian life, which is a belief strongly held by Catholics and Orthodox, but formally denied by Protestants, who hold that only Scripture is an infallible authority (what is known as *sola Scriptura*, "Bible alone").

As a Catholic convert, whose former biggest objection to Catholicism, by far, was the notion of an infallible Church or pope, I understand this viewpoint, but I thoroughly reject it now. As an introduction to the topic, I'd like to highlight three biblical passages that teach a very strong view of the authority of the Christian, or Catholic, Church.

> **Matthew 16:18-19**: And I tell you, you are Peter, and on this rock I will build my church, and the powers of death

Three Arguments for the Authority of the Church

> shall not prevail against it. I will give you the keys of the kingdom of heaven, and whatever you bind on earth shall be bound in heaven, and whatever you loose on earth shall be loosed in heaven.

This is also a key passage for the defense of the papacy, but that is a separate topic. Here I want to note that there is such a thing in the Bible as "the Church" and that it was established by Jesus Christ Himself as His own Church. Some comedian once made a wisecrack about there being "only one *the* Church." He spoke the truth.

St. Peter and the other apostles (of whom bishops and priests are successors) were given the power to bind and loose: Jewish rabbinical terms for penance (binding) and forgiveness extended by a representative of God (loosing). These decisions corresponded with the decrees or will of heaven itself (that is, God). Therefore, such power is indicative of a strong view of the authority of the Church.

The third notable element in this passage is the concept of the "powers of death" not being able to prevail against the Church. This means that the Church (not just individual Christians, but the collective entity) will always emerge victorious in her spiritual battles. The King James Version renders the phrase "powers of death" as "gates of hell." This brings to mind a great image of the Church breaking through, conquering the gates of hell itself and overcoming evil and Satan.

> **Acts 16:4**: As they went on their way through the cities, they delivered to them for observance the decisions which had been reached by the apostles and elders who were at Jerusalem.

Proving the Catholic Faith Is Biblical

This verse is often overlooked in discussions about authority in Christianity. St. Paul didn't simply hand out Bibles, nor did he preach the gospel only on his evangelistic journeys. He also proclaimed an authoritative Church decision, made at the Jerusalem Council, which is described in Acts 15:1-30.

What happened there was not "Bible alone" or individual Christians and the Holy Spirit, independent of other Christians, but very clearly a strong *Church* authority. The "apostles and elders" (Acts 15:6), representing the "whole church" (Acts 15:22) gathered, much as bishops in our time got together at the Second Vatican Council (1962-1965).

The main question they dealt with was whether Gentile Christian converts were required to be circumcised and to observe the entire Jewish Law. The Church in her council decided that it was *not* necessary, with the participants confidently proclaiming, "[I]t has seemed good to the Holy Spirit and to us." The Holy Spirit guided the process (see John 16:13).

St. Paul then went out and proclaimed what the council (including him) had decided, to be observed as a binding decree. If that's not Church authority, it's difficult to imagine what would be. If God approved of such Church-wide decisions in the early Church, why not also today? Why would that cease? It makes no sense to argue that it all went away and that we were left to fend for ourselves as mere individuals.

1 Timothy 3:15: the household of God, which is the church of the living God, the pillar and bulwark of the truth.

Truth is truth. It cannot be error, by its very essence and definition. How can truth's foundation or pillar or bulwark or ground be something *less* than total truth (since truth itself contains no

Three Arguments for the Authority of the Church

falsehoods, untruths, lies, or errors)? It cannot. It's impossible, as a straightforward matter of logic and plain observation. A stream cannot rise above its source.

What is built on a foundation cannot be *greater* than the foundation. If it were, the whole structure would collapse. If an elephant stood on the shoulders of a man as its foundation, that foundation would collapse. The base of a skyscraper has to hold the weight above it. It can't be weaker than that which is built upon it. The foundations of a suspension bridge over a river have to be strong enough to hold up that bridge. They can't possibly be weaker than the bridge, or the structure would collapse.

Therefore, we must conclude that if the Church is the *foundation* of truth, the Church *must* be infallible, since truth is infallible, and the foundation cannot be *less* great or strong than that which is built on it. Truth cannot be built on any degree of error whatever, because that would make the foundation weaker than the superstructure above it.

Accordingly, given the above biblical passages and many others, the Catholic "three-legged stool" rule of faith may be defined in the following way:

> In the biblical (and historic Catholic) view the inspired, infallible Bible is interpreted by an infallible, divinely guided Church, which in turn infallibly interprets and formulates the true doctrinal (apostolic) tradition.

9

Calling Catholic Priests *Father*

This is one of those garden-variety objections to Catholicism that come up so often. Like many such contra-Catholic arguments, it seems to have a plausibility at first glance. But on closer examination, the alleged difficulty vanishes. As so often is the case, this objection arises from an ignorance of the different forms of language in the Bible and of the importance of context. Critics of the Catholic Church frequently misunderstand both factors.

Matthew 23:9: And call no man your father on earth, for you have one Father, who is in heaven.

That seems straightforward enough, doesn't it? How do Catholics get around this? Are we wantonly disregarding and disobeying a direct command of our Lord Jesus?

No, not at all. Jesus was simply using the common Hebrew teaching method of exaggeration or hyperbole. This is common in, for example, the book of Proverbs. Here are several other instances of the same sort of thing:

Matthew 7:3: Why do you see the speck that is in your brother's eye, but do not notice the log that is in your own eye?

Calling Catholic Priests *Father*

> **Matthew 18:9**: And if your eye causes you to sin, pluck it out and throw it away; it is better for you to enter life with one eye than with two eyes to be thrown into the hell of fire.
>
> **Matthew 19:24**: Again I tell you, it is easier for a camel to go through the eye of a needle than for a rich man to enter the kingdom of God
>
> **Matthew 23:24**: You blind guides, straining out a gnat and swallowing a camel!
>
> **Luke 14:26**: If any one comes to me and does not hate his own father and mother and wife and children and brothers and sisters, yes, and even his own life, he cannot be my disciple.

Jesus was making the point that God the Father is the ultimate source of all authority. He said this during the course of rebuking the Pharisees for spiritual pride (Matt. 23:2-10). Those who try to reason in this way fail to see that, taken literally, Jesus' command would prohibit *all* uses of the word *father*, even in reference to biological fathers. Since that is an absurd outcome, it is clear that the statement cannot be taken in an absolute sense.

Such a sweeping prohibition clearly isn't what Jesus had in mind, since He uses the term *father* many times (and thus was not even following His own command, if the criticism is correct):

> **Matthew 15:4**: For God commanded, "Honor your father and your mother," and, "He who speaks evil of father or mother, let him surely die."

Matthew 19:5: For this reason a man shall leave his father and mother and be joined to his wife, and the two shall become one flesh.

Matthew 21:31: Which of the two did the will of his father?

Luke 16:24: And he called out, "Father Abraham, have mercy upon me." (cf. Luke 16:27, 30)

John 8:56: Your father Abraham rejoiced that he was to see my day; he saw it and was glad.

St. Stephen, St. Paul, and St. James use the term *father*:

Acts 7:2: And Stephen said: "Brethren and fathers, hear me. The God of glory appeared to our father Abraham."

Romans 4:12: the father of the circumcised ... our father Abraham.

Romans 4:16-17: Abraham ... is the father of us all, as it is written, "I have made you the father of many nations."

Romans 9:10: And not only so, but also when Rebecca had conceived children by one man, our forefather Isaac.

1 Corinthians 4:15: For though you have countless guides in Christ, you do not have many fathers. For I became your father in Christ Jesus through the gospel.

Philippians 2:22: But Timothy's worth you know, how as a son with a father he has served with me in the gospel.

James 2:21: Was not Abraham our father justified by works, when he offered his son Isaac upon the altar?

Calling Catholic Priests *Father*

It's a standard rule in hermeneutics (the interpretation of Scripture) that we interpret less clear passages of the Bible in light of passages relatively more clear. This is a classic case. What seemed so simple at first is shown to be a more complex, hyperbolic saying that can't possibly be taken literally in light of the abundant related scriptural data.

Jesus could not contradict Himself, nor could His apostles blatantly disregard or be unfamiliar with His teaching (right in inspired Scripture!). Therefore, the objection to calling Catholic priests *father* must be discarded, as a misguided nonstarter.

10

We Believe *All* That the Church Teaches

We call these doctrines that all Catholics must accept *de fide* (or, in some cases, *ex cathedra*) dogmas. In a nutshell, although there are fine (sometimes *very* fine) distinctions that can be drawn, Catholics are obliged, in the nature of the case, to accept all that the Church teaches.

It's an act of faith to accept that the Catholic Church is the one true Church established by Jesus Christ, historically continuous, universal, specially protected by the Holy Spirit for the purpose of passing down the apostolic deposit.

Because we accept this in faith as Catholics, it is required that we accept *all* that the Church teaches. To do that is itself a result of supernatural grace from God.

Protestants don't look at it that way because, first of all, they deny that the Church is infallible. Once one does that, it is a completely new rule of faith. For Protestants, this rule is *sola Scriptura*, or the idea that Scripture is the only infallible source of faith.

Therefore, it is very difficult for Protestants to accept the notion of submitting to a Church's teaching in faith, because for them, no Church has it completely right; only the Bible

We Believe *All* That the Church Teaches

does that. They often see this as virtually a violation of people's right to think for themselves or a violation of one's conscience.

It is neither. Rather, it is a recognition of our limitations, of something higher than ourselves, established by God, and of a Christian faith that includes acknowledgment of an authoritative, infallible Church. It takes faith, and faith is a supernatural gift granted by God through His grace and the assistance of the Holy Spirit. It's not *mere* reason but can be *supported* by reason, like all Christian dogma.

Some Protestants use the word *dogma*, but they generally prefer the word *doctrine*. To the extent that they are serious about historical Christian doctrine, Protestants do, of course, require a set of beliefs, too — just not as many as Catholics do. I always use the example of Calvinists. A truly Calvinist denomination (Presbyterian, Reformed, in their traditional forms and belief structures) would not allow a member to deny the five tenets of TULIP:

Total depravity
Unconditional election
Limited atonement
Irresistible grace
Perseverance of the saints

Disbelief in even two or three would not be permitted. They would no longer be considered members of the denomination, in terms of adherence to the creed of the group.

There are always people who join groups but disagree on some of the tenets of those groups. Catholics are not literally disallowed to have doubts and uncertainties (the Church is not simplistic or naive about such things), but they are supposed to accept *in faith* all that the Church teaches, and must certainly

Proving the Catholic Faith Is Biblical

not openly oppose it, whether they fully understand everything or not.

As an analogy from my Protestant days, I attended Assemblies of God churches for four years, but I disagreed with one of the 16 Fundamental Truths that everyone in the denomination was required to adhere to: the one (actually a combination of numbers 7 and 8) asserting that everyone had to speak in tongues in order to receive the "enduement of power." This I felt to be expressly contrary to Paul's teaching about tongues, where he says that not all speak in tongues (1 Cor. 12:30). Because of this, I never became a member. I was simply being honest, saying in effect: "I don't accept all sixteen truths that I am supposed to accept, so I won't become a member, but I agree with almost everything else taught."[1]

The Catholic Church doesn't expect everyone to have perfect faith or knowledge and to understand fully every jot and tittle. But the Church expects a humble submission to that which has been established and held from the beginning (with development of doctrine and increased understanding along the way).

There are always, despite all these considerations, people who are *in* a group but not totally *of* it. Many times, they don't properly *understand* the teachings of their own group. Other times, they do fully understand, and disagree, as I did in the Assemblies of God. I did what I felt was the only honest thing and did not

---

[1] Actually, looking at those truths again, I see that I didn't realize that number 12, on divine healing, is as sweeping as it is. It almost promises a healing for any true believer, which is dangerously false teaching that has caused untold misery and suffering and deaths in many cases, because people were misunderstanding how biblical healing works and how often it should be expected.

We Believe *All* That the Church Teaches

become a member, because that would have entailed ostensible agreement with a tenet that I did not accept. It would have been dishonest.

To make fairly simple and practical this concept of accepting all that the Church teaches, Catholics are not at liberty to disagree with, for example, what is included in the *Catechism of the Catholic Church*. It was promulgated under Pope John Paul II in 1992, accompanied by the Apostolic Constitution *Fidei Depositum*, which stated in part:

> The *Catechism of the Catholic Church*, which I approved 25 June last and the publication of which I today order by virtue of my Apostolic Authority, is a statement of the Church's faith and of catholic doctrine, attested to or illumined by Sacred Scripture, the Apostolic Tradition and the Church's Magisterium. I declare it to be a sure norm for teaching the faith and thus a valid and legitimate instrument for ecclesial communion....
>
> Therefore, I ask all the Church's Pastors and the Christian faithful to receive this catechism in a spirit of communion and to use it assiduously in fulfilling their mission of proclaiming the faith and calling people to the Gospel life. This catechism is given to them that it may be a sure and authentic reference text for teaching catholic doctrine and particularly for preparing local catechisms. It is also offered to all the faithful who wish to deepen their knowledge of the unfathomable riches of salvation (cf. *Eph* 3:8). It is meant to support ecumenical efforts that are moved by the holy desire for the unity of all Christians, showing carefully the content and wondrous harmony of the catholic faith. The *Catechism of the Catholic Church*,

lastly, is offered to every individual who asks us to give an account of the hope that is in us (cf. *1 Pt* 3:15) and who wants to know what the Catholic Church believes.[2]

---

[2] Pope St. John Paul II, Apostolic constitution *Fidei Depositum*, October 11, 1992, no. 3.

11

The Claim to Be the
One True Church

I find it noteworthy that the Catholic Church is far and away the most controversial, hated, despised Christian body (as Jesus predicted that His disciples would be). I regard that as strikingly analogous to the reactions to both Jesus and the early Christians. Radical truth claims have a way of creating controversy and strong opinions one way or the other.

The deeper question is: Would we expect *a priori* (in attempting to step back from our "sectarian" vantage points and looking at this issue with as much theoretical objectivity as we can muster) that the claims of the Christian Church (however it is defined) would cause such a controversial, polarizing reaction, or would we expect the one true Church (assuming that this is a valid, biblical claim and category) to elicit yawns and "ho hums" (or even laughter, as the case may be)? Clearly, the actual reaction was always closer to the former.

I think it is significant, then, that it is the Catholic Church's claims that always seem to be the focus of controversy. The Church is accused of all sorts of things, precisely because she is confident (or, triumphalistic, from a more cynical viewpoint) enough to make the claim in the first place—one that appears to me to be a rather routine, particularly Pauline one, in Holy Scripture.

In other words, the claim itself is the bare minimum prerequisite for being considered a contender for what the claim asserts. Most other Christians, meanwhile, want either to avoid it (a sort of ethereal "ecumenism") or to let it die the death of a thousand qualifications (settling for the unbiblical, anti-incarnational notion of the "invisible church," et cetera).

How does one determine what actually represents sacred tradition, if this is not determined by some authoritative Church? The problem is that, on one hand, mere private judgment is exercised (which has a host of difficulties, both biblically and historically, not to mention logically). On the other, the historical ecclesiological claim of being the one true Church cannot plausibly be made by anyone other than the Catholic Church.

That gets us right back to the rival claims and whether they are qualitatively equivalent. I say they are not, and I say that without the slightest trace of "triumphalism." I simply believe that no Church other than the Catholic Church can make this claim without massive self-contradiction or such a lack of plausibility as to make it impossible even to set forth the claim without running into a host of difficulties that are unable to be defended rationally.

Once this is understood (I accepted it after having read Newman's *Essay on the Development of Christian Doctrine*), it is seen that the choice is not so much the best one, but rather, the only *plausible* one. If difficulties with individual Catholic dogmas remain, one has to realize that one's private judgment is insufficient to judge such a massive thing as the Catholic Church, with the overwhelming weight of tradition behind it.

The Claim to Be the One True Church

One has to submit at some point, in faith, as a matter of intellectual duty and in obedience to the leading of grace and faith. Note that I don't say that everyone understands Catholicism sufficiently to make such a commitment, and there are many reasons for that. My case here doesn't require a judgment that all non-Catholics are dishonest or insincere in their convictions (absolutely not!).

But I am saying that once one grasps these issues (*if* in fact how I described them above is the correct way of analyzing these matters), it is incumbent on him to either become a Catholic or to set forth some compelling counterargument as to why he should not.

Much of the hostility toward the Catholic Church comes from (in my opinion) the reaction against her claim to be the one true Church. I don't think there is any question that the Church receives more flak for her claims than anyone else. As the Church make more claims than anyone else in the first place, this is to be expected, I suppose. But it is not insignificant.

12

On Whether God Would Protect His Church from Error

In a discussion with an Anglican and two other men who were possibly also Anglican, but in any event, not Catholics, I asked them which of these statements they thought was true:

1. God is *unable* to preserve Christian doctrine without error throughout history by means of (in and of themselves, without His aid) fallen, imperfect, fallible men and an imperfect Church run by such men (i.e., sinners). Since you seem to think He was unable to do that with the Bible, too, I suppose you would affirm this, but I'm asking, to be sure.

2. God was, of course, *able* to do this if He chose to (being omnipotent), but He chose *not* to do so.

"If you chose number 1," I asked them, "why do you believe that? Is it because you deny God's omnipotence? If you chose number 2, why do you think God would not protect true theology from corruption, especially in light of the biblical teaching that the Holy Spirit will guide us into all truth?"

One of them responded that it was "highly presumptuous" to speculate about what God should or would do or why He does it.

Whether God Would Protect His Church from Error

I don't agree at all—not when what He does or doesn't do is a function of His omnipotence, and if it is indicated in Scripture as harmonious with what we in fact see Him doing, and when it involves something of high importance to the well-being of souls.

Basically my argument here was a subtle variation of a *reductio ad absurdum*: I am working from what we *know* to more *speculative* things. I don't regard it as a species of epistemology at all; rather, it is an exercise in consistency of logic combined with data from revelation that Protestants and Catholics hold in common. And, as usual, I am probing premises, because I think they have been insufficiently scrutinized in this instance.

I continued: "If we grant that He allows error, how much error do you think He allows? You give a nod to the Holy Spirit's guidance below, so do you think it goes a certain distance and then we are on our own? That wasn't the view at the council of Jerusalem or St. Paul's. Everything was quite certain then and 'seemed good to the Holy Spirit and to us' (Acts 15:28). But that was before the days when denominations and division had to be rationalized as somehow remotely sanctioned by Holy Scripture."

I deliberately compared this situation to the infallible, inspired Bible, because most orthodox Christians throughout history have held a very high view of Scripture. God did that via sinful men, so the question becomes: "Why should doctrine or creeds be any different?"

It's a very serious (and I believe, important) question and a matter of trust in God and acceptance of what seems fairly obvious (at least to me) in Scripture; i.e., a matter of revelation, which exists apart from a necessary epistemological rationale. We accept what it says in faith. One could say it comes down to hermeneutics, too, since what I see in the Bible seems perfectly harmonious with an authoritative Church, preserved from error.

Proving the Catholic Faith Is Biblical

I never received anywhere near direct or serious counterarguments to my questions, but one can only try. If we keep asking relevant questions and receive no better answers than what we believe Catholicism provides, to us this is evidence of the fullness of truth within Catholicism and the incoherence and implausibility of alternatives.

13

Are Church Councils More Authoritative Than Popes?

THE CHURCH[3]
The council is a higher authority than a pope.
Rome's theory of popes presiding over councils is a self-serving late invention.

Initial reply
In the only Church council recorded in Scripture: the Jerusalem council, Peter presided, and the Catholic Church has simply followed that biblical model.

Extensive reply
The council of Jerusalem (Acts 15:1-29) gives us an example in God's revelation, the Bible, of how Church affairs might proceed. The topic at hand was whether the Gentiles had to follow the Mosaic Law completely, including all of its rituals and ceremonies. It seems clear that Peter, the leader of the apostles, presided

---

[3] This chapter is written in the format of my book *The One-Minute Apologist* (Manchester, New Hampshire: Sophia Institute Press, 2007), vaguely reminiscent of St. Thomas Aquinas's *Summa Theologica*.

over this council. It was not without a leader; nor was James, the bishop of Jerusalem, the leader, as some maintain. The internal evidence in favor of this interpretation is as follows:

1. St. Peter was the first to speak definitively, and with authority, "after there had been much debate" (Acts 15:7).

2. Peter claimed authority in a special way: "Brethren, you know that in the early days God made choice among you, that by my mouth the Gentiles should hear the word of the Gospel and believe" (Acts 15:7).

3. Peter sternly rebuked the opposing view of strict observance of ceremonial law: "Now therefore why do you make trial of God by putting a yoke upon the neck of the disciples which neither our fathers nor we have been able to bear?" (Acts 15:10).

4. After Peter spoke, the debate was essentially over, and "all the assembly kept silence" (Acts 15:12).

5. Those who talked after Peter did not disagree with his decision, and merely confirmed it (Acts 15:12-21).

6. St. James did not hand down the main decree or add anything new to what Peter had already proclaimed. He started out by noting, "Simeon [Peter] has related …" (Acts 15:14).

7. James states, "Therefore my judgment …", but this does not prove that he presided, as anyone could say that (similar to saying, "My opinion is …"). The judgment was reached by consensus ("it seemed good to the apostles and elders, with the whole church" [Acts 15:22];

Are Councils More Authoritative Than Popes?

"it has seemed good to us, having come to one accord" [Acts 15:25]; "it has seemed good to the Holy Spirit and to us" [Acts 15:28; cf. 16:4]). This, too, is exactly like Catholic councils throughout history: they decide matters as a group, yet the pope presides. Nothing in this text suggests other than that Peter was the leader.

8. St. Paul is not shown as having any special authority in the council (many think he had more authority in the early Church than Peter). Instead, we learn that he and Barnabas "were appointed to go up to Jerusalem to the apostles and elders about this question" (Acts 15:2). Paul and Barnabas merely give report of their experiences (Acts 15:12), and then they are sent by the council to report what had been decided (Acts 15:25, 30; 16:4).

Objection

But the Catholic view of papal infallibility and popes presiding over councils was not made infallible dogma until 1870 (First Vatican Council), so it was a novelty.

Reply to Objection

That doesn't mean that this state of affairs was not already in place. It had been explicitly proclaimed and exercised since the early centuries of the Church, and we already see it in the Bible (as above). As just one example of many such statements from Church historians, the Anglican patristics expert J.N.D. Kelly, wrote:

> By the middle of the fifth century the Roman church had established, *de jure* as well as *de facto*, a position of primacy in the West, and the papal claims to supremacy over all

Proving the Catholic Faith Is Biblical

bishops in Christendom had been formulated in precise terms.... The student tracing the history of the times ... cannot fail to be impressed by the skill and persistence with which the Holy See was continually advancing and consolidating its claims.... It was easy to draw the inference that the unique authority which Rome in fact enjoyed, and which the popes saw concentrated in their persons and their office, was no more than the fulfillment of the divine plan.[4]

Oxford Church historian R. W. Southern wrote:

No one in the West denied that the pope possessed all the authority of St Peter over the church. The derivation of the pope's authority seemed one of the clearest facts of history. The descent of this authority could be traced step by step from the earliest days without any of the shadows of ambiguity or ignorance that trouble a modern observer.... From the beginning St Peter and his successors could be seen at work directing the church, instituting ceremonies, defining discipline, founding bishoprics. This scheme of things had the same unambiguous clarity as the generations of mankind from Adam.[5]

---

[4] J.N.D. Kelly, *Early Christian Doctrines*, rev. ed. (San Francisco: HarperCollins, 1978), 417.
[5] R. W. Southern, *Western Society and the Church in the Middle Ages* (Baltimore: Penguin Books, 1970), 94.

14

Catholic Priestly Celibacy

PROTESTANT. Enforced celibacy of the priesthood is unscriptural.

DAVE ARMSTRONG. Thus you prove you are of the sort who couldn't receive the saying of Jesus when He said:

> **Matthew 19:12**: For there are eunuchs who have been so from birth, and there are eunuchs who have been made eunuchs by men, and there are eunuchs who have made themselves eunuchs for the sake of the kingdom of heaven. He who is able to receive this, let him receive it.

PROTESTANT. The key word is *enforced*. Matthew 19:12 speaks of voluntary celibacy.

D. A. It's not enforced if we simply choose from among those men who have been called to it. The Catholic Church (i.e., Latin Rite, because not all our rites have this requirement) says, "We want our priests to come from that class of men who have been called by God to be celibate." This is quite biblical. Paul talks about single men who can offer undistracted devotion to the Lord, in 1 Corinthians 7. So we say: "We want to draw our priests from that pool." Completely biblical, completely sensible.

PROTESTANT. So, you tell a man who is married, or desires to be married, and wants to give his life to ministry, "Tough luck, buddy"?

D. A. No. We say, "Many of our rites allow married priests; perhaps you would consider one of those, or the diaconate." There are many ministries in the Church; lots of things to do. I am a married apologist and evangelist and have been so full-time for almost thirteen years. Marriage hasn't stopped me from following my calling.

In any event, it does no good to run down a way of life that is so highly honored in Scripture (John the Baptist, Jesus, most of the disciples, the eunuchs Jesus refers to, the single men referred to in 1 Corinthians 7).

Protestants who argue as you do usually object to celibacy because they think celibacy is impossible (as Luther and Calvin virtually argued). They don't have enough faith in God's power and grace. We do. Those of you who don't "get" it, don't get those passages and examples in the Bible. You don't follow the teachings of *all* of the Bible.

15

The Celibate Priesthood as a Higher Calling

How do we tie the married priesthood (in Eastern Catholicism and Orthodoxy) into the evangelical counsels? Doesn't the Church teach that it is a higher calling to renounce marriage for the sake of ministry (and yes, "undistracted devotion to the Lord": 1 Corinthians 7)?

Doesn't the Church teach that consecrated virginity or celibacy is a higher state of life than marriage, per the evangelical counsels? My understanding is that it does. If that is true in general, then I submit that the general principle would apply to priests as a particular manifestation of it.

It's like abstinence and fasting, which are spiritually helpful. Thus, if one gives up marriage and its gifts in order to be more fully devoted to the Lord, that too is a higher state.

In other words, married priesthood is very good; celibate priesthood is better.

Married folks can do much in the Church. I serve the Church as a full-time apologist. But I could do a lot *more* apologetics and evangelism if I were single.

St. Paul was a priest and a model for us. Now, in 1 Corinthians 9:5, he states: "Do we not have the right to be accompanied by a wife, as the other apostles and the brothers of the Lord and

Cephas?" And he goes on to argue in the same passage that the spiritual worker earns his wages, is worthy of his wages. But he also writes:

> **1 Corinthians 9:15-19**: But I have made no use of any of these rights, nor am I writing this to secure any such provision. For I would rather die than have any one deprive me of my ground for boasting. For if I preach the gospel, that gives me no ground for boasting. For necessity is laid upon me. Woe to me if I do not preach the gospel! For if I do this of my own will, I have a reward; but if not of my own will, I am entrusted with a commission. What then is my reward? Just this: that in my preaching I may make the gospel free of charge, not making full use of my right in the gospel. For though I am free from all men, I have made myself a slave to all, that I might win the more.

He specifically renounces marriage and even remuneration, although he says he has a right to both, for the sake of the gospel. Now, based on that, I conclude that it is more commendable and "higher" for St. Paul to have done that, compared with the next priest over who does *not* do it. It's a higher calling for him to renounce having a wife, so that he may "win the more," as he says.

Given Paul's argument, can we say that what he did was no higher or more commendable in his calling than the others who didn't take his "extra" step (the evangelical counsels)? And, of course, St. Peter and others also left their wives for the express sake of ministry. We know that because it is expressly *stated*:

> **Luke 18:28-30**: And Peter said, "Lo, we have left our homes and followed you." And he said to them, "Truly, I say to you, there is no man who has left house or wife or

The Celibate Priesthood as a Higher Calling

brothers or parents or children, for the sake of the kingdom of God, who will not receive manifold more in this time, and in the age to come eternal life."

We know Peter was married. He left "everything." Unless he was already a widower, he renounced marriage for the sake of his ministry. Why? Why should he do that, or have to do it in any sense? Why didn't Jesus say, "Well, hey, you can be married and come along with us, Simon. No problem!"? I say it was because it was presupposed that singleness was a superior state from which to engage in full-time Christian ministry and (eventually) priesthood.

I don't deny that a married priest can be a great priest. I know some wonderful married priests myself, even in the Latin Rite. But I deny that celibacy is not a higher calling than marriage, based on:

- the evangelical counsels
- Paul's reasoning in 1 Corinthians 7 and 9
- Jesus' reasoning about the voluntary eunuchs for the sake of the kingdom (Matt. 19)
- the motif of leaving one's family, including, seemingly, wives, for the sake of the kingdom

If St. Paul's was a "higher calling," that seals my argument as to the higher calling of a celibate priesthood. If it was a higher calling for *him*, then it is a higher calling for *any* priest who does the same (since Paul often says that we should imitate him). So the Latin Rite says, "We are drawing exclusively from that pool of men who have already been called by God to the celibate life, and we think that is very good—preferable—for the sake of undistracted devotion."

The example of Paul in 1 Corinthians 9 specifically ties in the priesthood and celibacy, because he was a priest. Thus, advocates for the Eastern Catholic or Orthodox system of mostly married priests can't retort that 1 Corinthians 7 isn't about priests (or that the eunuch of Matthew 19 isn't about priests). It's a clear example of a priest's saying he has renounced marriage for the sake of ministry. It seems plainly "higher" to me.

Based on how St. Paul argues it, he appears to assume that it would apply widely as a spiritual principle. Paul says that he specifically renounced what was his "right" in order to produce more spiritual fruit: to "win all the more." It's a direct causation for him: voluntarily renouncing remuneration and the married life means more fruit in his ministry.

16

A New Argument for Mandatory Priestly Celibacy?

I was curious about the approximate percentage of Eastern Orthodox and Eastern Catholic priests who are celibate (i.e., those who are celibate in an environment where a married priesthood is allowed). My thought was that if celibacy is so valued in "non-Latin" Christianity, as is claimed, we should expect to see a significant number (maybe one-quarter?, one-third?) of celibate clergy (since they are given the choice). If not, then it seems reasonable to conclude that it is relatively *less* valued, so that among these priests, the percentage who opt for marriage would be scarcely distinguishable from that of the general public.

And that in turn (if true) would be another argument in favor of mandatory celibacy, since if it isn't required, then what Paul recommended as a preferred state for clergy will quickly become a rarity. Human nature seems to teach us that what is very difficult usually won't be chosen unless it is mandatory in some sense. Hence, we have the explicitly biblical notion of the evangelical counsels.

Among statistics I could find, I discovered that about 91 percent (575 of 630) of active Greek Orthodox priests in the United

States were married. According to another study, 93 percent of all Orthodox priests in America were married. Assuming the accuracy of this survey, about one in ten Orthodox priests (at least those in America) feel called to a celibate state.

Therefore, I would conclude from the statistics that celibacy is greatly undervalued in Orthodoxy among the class of clergy; otherwise it would be practiced by more than only 7 to 10 percent of all Orthodox clergy. The state in life that St. Paul taught was preferable in terms of undistracted devotion to the Lord occurs far less among Eastern Orthodox clergy, because it is not required. The result becomes like the situation in Protestantism: clergy are allowed to marry, so virtually all do, and those who don't are too often regarded with suspicion. I think this is human nature: if an easier path is allowed, almost all take it, whereas difficult things need to be required.

Latin rite Catholicism thinks celibacy is so praiseworthy and honorable that it chooses to draw its priests almost exclusively from the class of men who agree with Paul and follow one of the evangelical counsels as regards their own calling in life. I've never understood the objection to this (even when I was an evangelical Protestant I understood the reasoning of it).

What would be the reply to this line of argumentation? One "solution" or middle course (I don't advocate it myself; I'm just thinking theoretically) might be to have a clergy that is (deliberately, by requirement) 50 percent celibate and 50 percent married, so that both callings are equally valued in practice. Otherwise it seems to be an all-or-nothing situation: 99 percent celibate clergy (a few exceptions for Anglican clergy converts, et cetera) or 90 to 93 percent married clergy. If the statistics are similar in Eastern Catholic clergy (as I strongly suspect will be the case), my point is strengthened.

A New Argument for Priestly Celibacy?

An Orthodox Christian in a Facebook thread denied that there was an innate relationship between celibacy and the priesthood. But if this is so, why (if there is not at least a strong correlation) were Jesus and all the disciples either not married or married (like Peter) with an agreement to leave their wives for the sake of ministry, with Jesus actually referring to those who have left wives or families for His sake (Luke 18:29)?

Between that and St. Paul's strong teaching in 1 Corinthians 7, do we not see a sort of biblical/apostolic preference toward the state of celibacy for clergy? Of course, the ones who are celibate for the sake of the kingdom come from a small "pool," but then priests are very extraordinary and exceptional men, so I would fully expect them to come from a small and very special subclass of men in the first place.

There are plenty of opportunities for married ministry. One can be a deacon or a director of religious education or a youth pastor or a teacher in a Catholic school. These roles don't require looking after an entire parish. It's very difficult to balance that and a family. Just ask children of Protestant pastors how that often works out. People can do only so much.

Of course no one should be a celibate priest unless he is called to it. This is self-evident. Existing problems do not cast doubt on the principle — only on the selection process. We draw our priests from a smaller group of men than Orthodoxy does. The goal and task is to find holy men who truly are called to the priesthood and/or to celibacy. This is of supreme importance, given the sexual scandals and heterodoxy that have occurred.

I don't see why the Latin system of required priestly celibacy should so often be disparaged. There is biblical support for it. Catholicism as a whole has both traditions (since Eastern

Catholicism allows a married clergy) and values diversity of opinion and practice.

It all goes back to the selection process. If we agree that celibate priests and married priests are both valid, then the Catholic (Latin) Church has to make sure that candidates for the priesthood are called to celibacy, and Orthodoxy has to make sure that a married priest can handle both family and Church responsibilities. These are two very different sets of capabilities and personal needs.

17

Works Can Be Good or Bad, Just Like Traditions

The author of Hebrews makes this distinction:

Bad Works

> **Hebrews 6:1**: Therefore let us leave the elementary doctrine of Christ and go on to maturity, not laying again a foundation of repentance from dead works and of faith toward God.

> **Hebrews 9:14**: [H]ow much more shall the blood of Christ, who through the eternal Spirit offered himself without blemish to God, purify your conscience from dead works?

Good Works

> **Hebrews 6:10**: For God is not so unjust as to overlook your work and the love which you showed for his sake in serving the saints, as you still do.

> **Hebrews 10:24**: [L]et us consider how to stir up one another to love and good works.

Hebrews 13:20-21: May the God of peace ... equip you with everything good that you may do his will, working in you that which is pleasing in his sight, through Jesus Christ; to whom be glory for ever and ever. Amen.

Revelation 3:2 offers a similar treatment: "I have not found your works perfect in the sight of my God."

The phrase "good works" is also found in Matthew 5:16; John 10:32; Acts 9:36; and Ephesians 2:10.

18

Faith and Works

Isaiah 1 provides a case study in taking passages out of context to bolster preconceived notions. Ironically, it was a longtime Baptist friend of mine who called my attention to this. (He's a good Protestant—in no "danger" of becoming Catholic—but unlike many Protestants, he doesn't try to omit the importance of good works in the Christian life.) The passage usually cited by Protestants is Isaiah 1:18:

> *Come now, let us reason together,*
> *says the LORD:*
> *though your sins are like scarlet,*
> *they shall be as white as snow;*
> *though they are red like crimson,*
> *they shall become like wool.*

This is reminiscent of Psalm 51:2, 7, 9-10 and King David's repentance:

> *Wash me thoroughly from my iniquity,*
> *and cleanse me from my sin! . . .*
> *Purge me with hyssop, and I shall be clean;*
> *wash me, and I shall be whiter than snow. . . .*

Proving the Catholic Faith Is Biblical

*Hide thy face from my sins,
and blot out all my iniquities.
Create in me a clean heart, O God,
and put a new and right spirit within me.*

Protestants (of a certain sort) don't and won't hesitate to cite the Old Testament as authoritative if they think a passage *supports* their theology. When it doesn't, they tend to dismiss it as irrelevant, because, well, it is the *Old* Testament. Quite often (if not, typically), evangelical and Reformed and fundamentalist Protestants cite Isaiah 1:18 in isolation as a prooftext for one-time justification or instant salvation, or both.

When we examine the context, we see that works are part and parcel of what is being dealt with. The immediate context is most striking (and jolting for those who hold to Protestant soteriology). Here are the two verses preceding Isaiah 1:18:

*Wash yourselves; make yourselves clean;
remove the evil of your doings
from before my eyes;
cease to do evil,
learn to do good;
seek justice,
correct oppression;
defend the fatherless,
plead for the widow. (cf. Isa. 1:23)*

Isn't it fascinating how God, through His prophet, includes the *actions of the penitent* in the whole equation? Protestants tell us nothing can be done by man prior to justification (what many of them equate with a "salvation" that can't ever be lost once truly granted). We agree with them, insofar as we are talking about

Faith and Works

initial justification or regeneration. Those are entirely works of God's grace, and this is the clear teaching of the Council of Trent. But then, the context of this passage doesn't fit into that scenario. Here, man is clearly *doing* something—quite a bit—and it can't be separated from God's pardon. Catholics simply say that it may be an instance of justification after the time of initial justification, because we don't think justification is a one-time thing. Protestants will have to offer some other explanation concerning the context or cease using Isaiah 1:18 as a prooftext for justification (as they define it).

God says, "Wash yourselves; make yourselves clean" and two verses later, we see the result: "your sins ... shall be as white as snow." But Protestants want to ignore all the actions of men in the overall passage. In Isaiah 1:17, God talks about a bunch of works: doing good, seeking justice, battling oppression, helping fatherless children and widows... How reminiscent this is of the judgment passages, where Jesus says that the key to salvation is not faith alone, but rather, works:

Matthew 25:34-36: Then the King will say to those at his right hand, "Come, O blessed of my Father, inherit the kingdom prepared for you from the foundation of the world; for I was hungry and you gave me food, I was thirsty and you gave me drink, I was a stranger and you welcomed me, I was naked and you clothed me, I was sick and you visited me, I was in prison and you came to me."

The same things (works and obedience) are seen in the two passages following 1:18:

If you are willing and obedient,
you shall eat the good of the land;

Proving the Catholic Faith Is Biblical

> *But if you refuse and rebel,*
> *you shall be devoured by the sword;*
> *for the mouth of the Lord has spoken.*

Everything is conditional. It's the furthest thing from an irrevocable, unconditional promise. The entire chapter is about the nation of Israel, but generally such passages are regarded as having a double application to the Christian believer (as God's "chosen," et cetera). How about Isaiah 1:27? Does it talk about faith alone as the prerequisite of justification and one-time salvation? Hardly:

> *Zion shall be redeemed by justice,*
> *and those in her who repent, by righteousness.*

Redeemed by "justice"? "Redeem" and "redemption" are good Protestant words, and they refer to *God's actions only*, not our own. But there it is in front of our face.

It's the same everywhere in the chapter. There is no respite for the Protestant who dares to read the whole thing, and to interpret 1:18 in context, rather than atomistically isolated, as if it were merely a saying on a poster, to be repeated without any examination.

> *Ah, sinful nation,*
> *a people laden with iniquity,*
> *offspring of evildoers,*
> *sons who deal corruptly!*
> *They have forsaken the Lord,*
> *they have despised the Holy One of Israel,*
> *they are utterly estranged.*

If Israel represents the individual sinner or the Christian, here we have a nation (by double application, person) that once

Faith and Works

knew the Lord but no longer does. You can't "forsake" something or someone without having formerly followed him or it. Yet by Calvinist and Baptist and evangelical "perseverance" and "eternal security" thinking, this is not *possible*. One can't fall away. Grace is irresistible, and election is unconditional. Thus we have to choose between what the Bible teaches and what *men* teach, in *contradiction* of it.

Under Catholic principles, on the other hand, no problem at all! Men can fall away from grace and be restored to it through repentance and absolution and additional justification. Our view is perfectly consistent with what we find here.

Prayer and worship and rituals and calling on God for salvation are worthless unless we repent from the heart and indicate it by our good works:

> *Bring no more vain offerings;*
> *incense is an abomination to me.*
> *New moon and sabbath and the calling of assemblies —*
> *I cannot endure iniquity and solemn assembly.*
> *Your new moons and your appointed feasts*
> *my soul hates;*
> *they have become a burden to me,*
> *I am weary of bearing them.*
> *When you spread forth your hands,*
> *I will hide my eyes from you;*
> *even though you make many prayers,*
> *I will not listen;*
> *your hands are full of blood.*

Here as everywhere in Scripture, faith and works are together. Man cooperates with God after receiving initial justification and regeneration (which come *entirely* by God's grace).

19

Belief in Jesus Requires Obedience to Him

John 3:36: He who believes in the Son has eternal life; he who does not obey the Son shall not see life, but the wrath of God rests upon him.

"Believes" here in the Greek original is *pistuo*, and the Greek for "does not obey" is *apeitheo*. Belief and obedience are, then, presented as essentially identical. To believe in Christ *is* to obey Him. To disobey Him is to be subject to God's wrath. St. Peter, in 1 Peter 2:7, makes the same comparison, with the same two Greek words. Thus, by this understanding, *pistuo* elsewhere in Scripture is harmonious with the Catholic view of infused justification.

Apeitheo (Strong's word no. 544) can indeed mean "disobey" or "disobedient" as *Strong's Concordance* notes. That's precisely why the Revised Standard Version translates it as "not obey" at John 3:36, whereas the King James Version (KJV) has "believeth not." But the KJV also translates it as "disobedient" in 1 Peter 2:7.

Many translators have thought that the usage here was the concept of disobedience and not merely the refusal to give

Belief in Jesus Requires Obedience to Him

assent. It was also translated "obeyeth not" in the revised version of the KJV. What do other translators think? Here are many non-Catholic versions that render the term in the sense of "disobey":

- **NEB, REB, NRSV, Goodspeed, Moffatt, TEV**: disobeys the Son
- **Living Bible**: don't believe and obey him
- **NIV**: rejects the Son
- **NASB**: does not obey the Son
- **Beck**: will not listen to the Son
- **Amplified**: disobeys — is unbelieving toward, refuses to trust in, disregards, is not subject to — the Son
- **CEV**: rejects him
- **ASV**: obeyeth not

Also, Gerhard Kittel's *Theological Dictionary of the New Testament* (one-volume edition) states that *apeitheo* in John 3:36 means "disobeying the Son" (p. 820). Cognate words *apeithes* and *apeitheia* mean "unworthy of belief," then "disobedient" and "disobedience," respectively (pp. 819-820).

As for *pistuo*, the work states:

[P]*isteuo* as "to obey." Heb. 11 stresses that to believe is to obey, as in the OT. Paul in Rom. 1:8; 1 th. 1:8 (cf. Rom 15:18; 16:19) shows, too, that believing means obeying. he speaks about the obedience of faith in Rom. 1:5, and cf. 10:3; 2 Cor. 9:13. (p. 854)

Since faith involves confession and obedience, it is a state as well as an act. ... There is a work of faith (1 Th. 1:3); it works by love (Gal. 5:6). This work stands in contrast to the works of the law. (p. 855)

The argument proceeds from language (the meaning of Greek words), context, internal parallelism, and cross reference or external parallelism.

20

Faith Calls for Confidence and Perseverance

RSV: For we share in Christ, if only we hold our first confidence firm to the end.

KJV: For we are made partakers of Christ, if we hold the beginning of our confidence steadfast unto the end.

Moffatt: For we only participate in Christ provided that we keep firm to the very end the confidence with which we started.

Revised Fundamentalist Version (tongue-in-cheek): For we believe in and proclaim Christ only if we make a firm one-time commitment and altar call with which we start and end.

The passage is a goldmine of Catholic theology. It starts out with a seeming allusion to theosis, or profound union with God: a doctrine emphasized by the Orthodox but perfectly Catholic and biblical as well. Then we have the conditional *if* and *only* in some versions: this union or final salvation occurs only if we continue to the end. It's not guaranteed and perfectly known henceforth, in an instant.

Proving the Catholic Faith Is Biblical

Then we have the notion of synergy or cooperation, coworking with God, by His grace. We have something to do; we're not passive. We have to keep firm and confident. Our starting proclamation has to be vigilantly maintained. Salvation is a process, not a moment.

To summarize:

1. Theosis.

2. Conditional salvation is based on whether we persevere in what we proclaim; not instant salvation.

3. Cooperation or colaboring with God and His grace in order to persevere.

4. Salvation is a process.

5. We are assured ("confident") of our salvation, yet we must laboriously keep and maintain such assurance.

6. In other words, salvation or being in God's good grace can be lost. That's what "if" and "only" and "keep firm" and "unto the end" are all about.

Neither eternal security, nor the Calvinist perseverance of the saints, nor a denial of human free will to cooperate in the salvation wrought ultimately (as both enabling and final cause) by God's grace, nor a bald assent of faith without action, nor any notion of instant, one-time salvation can be squared with this passage at all.

I'm not "coming up" with this; it's God's revelation. One can accept the teaching it gives us here and in many, many other places, or reject it, miserably slogging along with mere false traditions of men, made up out of whole cloth, rather than from the inspired Bible.

21

The "Unanswered" Prayers of Jesus

A Reformed Baptist (Calvinist) argued that if Christ in fact died for all men, rather than the elect only (as Calvinists hold), this would result in His interceding in heaven as high priest for those He knows (in His omniscience and perfect foreknowledge) will reject Him and go to hell.

It would then follow that His intercession failed, or (if there is any difference) was unanswered—an unthinkable state of affairs for God.

The reply to this is, I think, simple: yes, Christ's intercession failed, in the cases of those who went to hell, because human free will trumps even God's will (by God's own design). Hence, Calvinism denies free will as well (in effect, futilely to try to overcome this difficulty).

Once that goes, then whatever Jesus prays for in terms of men would inevitably happen, and that is what creates the intended supposed "dilemma" for the person who holds to universal atonement (as virtually all Christians besides Calvinists do).

God allows things to happen that go against His perfect will. The devil's (and demons') own fall from grace is an example. I imagine that Jesus, who is eternal, prayed to the Father for

Proving the Catholic Faith Is Biblical

Lucifer at one time, since he was God's greatest creation. The fall of man is another (most Calvinists no longer being Supralapsarian—which means believing that God preordained the Fall of man—though I have argued that Calvin himself was).

Jesus chose Judas to be His disciple. He prayed for him, no doubt, as He did for all the other disciples, but Judas's free will couldn't be overcome (lest it not be free will at all).

Here are two examples from Scripture of Jesus' willing one thing (and in one case, praying for it), and men willing another thing, and (guess what?) the rebellious will prevails:

> **Matthew 23:37**: O Jerusalem, Jerusalem, killing the prophets and stoning those who are sent to you! How often *would* I have gathered your children together as a hen gathers her brood under her wings, and you *would not*! (cf. Luke 13:34)

Jesus prayed specifically that His followers "may be one, even as we [He and the Father] are one" (John 17:11) and "that they may all be one; even as thou, Father, art in me, and I in thee" (John 17:21), and again, "one even as we are one, I in them and thou in me, that they may become perfectly one" (John 17:22-23).

Clearly, Christians fall far short (abominably short) of what Jesus intended for this prayer (again, out of our free will to sin and not follow His desires and commands), so it is equally plainly a failed prayer.

Jesus prayed that His disciples would be one. We're not. We will be one in heaven, but not on earth. His overall providence doesn't fail, because it incorporates within itself our free-will responses, including rejections of His perfect will. But individual prayers fail if their aim is not met: even for Jesus.

The "Unanswered" Prayers of Jesus

Likewise, God can't do some things, even though He is omnipotent. They have to be logically *possible*. For example, He can't make a square circle or make two plus two equal five. He can't obliterate Himself out of existence or make Himself noneternal.

This is what lies behind the old atheist challenge: "Can God make a rock so heavy that He couldn't lift it?" He cannot do so; not because He is not omnipotent (able to do all that is *possible* to do), but because no weight is too heavy for Him to "lift": therefore there is no such rock that He can create. It's *logical* impossibility; not a disproof of His omnipotence. But the atheist is counting on us not to recognize the necessary distinctions (or, more likely, he does not grasp them himself).

Jesus prayed, "My Father, if it be *possible*, let this cup pass from me; nevertheless, not as I will, but as thou wilt" (Matt. 26:39). But it *wasn't* possible, because some things aren't possible even for God. In this instance it wasn't possible for Jesus to avoid the Passion.

> **2 Peter 3:9**: The Lord is not slow about his promise as some count slowness, but is forbearing toward you, not wishing that any should perish, but that all should reach repentance.

But we know that not all reach repentance. Damned folks go to hell. We know that for sure because Scripture mentions it in several places (see, e.g., Matt. 5:22; 10:28; Matt. 23:33; 25:41).

Therefore, God's desire, which for Him is the same as a prayer because He knows all at once, is not fulfilled in its goal (the salvation of all). It can't be, given human free will, which He allowed to be present. God gives all men sufficient grace to be saved, but that can be rejected and is, *in fact*, by the reprobate.

Proving the Catholic Faith Is Biblical

Some try to argue that Jesus' prayer for Christian unity in John 17 is answered in heaven, but the context (which has nothing to do with perfection in heaven, but rather, life in this world, with all its problems) utterly rules that out as an explanation:

John 17:11: And now I am no more in the world, but *they are in the world*, and I am coming to thee. Holy Father, keep them in thy name, which thou hast given me, that they may be one, even as we are one.

John 17:15: I do not pray that thou shouldst take them out of the *world*, but that thou shouldst keep them from the evil one.

John 17:17: Sanctify them in the truth; thy word is truth.

No more sanctification takes place in heaven.

John 17:18: As thou didst send me into the world, so I have sent them into the *world*.

In each case, the context is in the world.

John 17:2: that they may all be one; even as thou, Father, art in me, and I in thee, that they also may be in us, so that the *world* may believe that thou hast sent me.

John 17:23: I in them and thou in me, that they may become perfectly one, so that the *world* may know that thou hast sent me and hast loved them even as thou hast loved me.

The previous two passages can't possibly apply to the afterlife, because they have to do with *witness*. If they are one in the world, the world will believe in Jesus as a result of observing them.

The "Unanswered" Prayers of Jesus

We thus conclude from the previous passages:

1. Can God will one thing without its coming to pass? Matthew 23:37 shows that this can indeed happen. So does 2 Peter 3:9, where God desires that none perish, yet many do and go to hell.

2. Can something that Jesus prays for not happen? John 17 shows this, and the Calvinist's exegesis is utterly implausible and takes no account of the entire repeated context, which has to do with the world, not the final state.

There are some things that even God can't do. He can't force a person to believe with his free will opposed, because the two notions are incompatible. But He can give everyone enough grace to be saved, and they have it in order to cooperate with their free will.

God doesn't predestine people to hell, though (only to heaven). That is Calvinist heresy. And so the people in hell run counter to God's desire (in Scripture) that none perish.

It was virtually impossible for Jesus' prayer in John 17 to have been realized, given human sin. By allowing human free will, God allows into the universe sins that are not in accord with His perfect will. And He can't make a man with free will unfree by forcing him to be good and righteous and nonrebellious.

22

St. John vs. John Calvin on Limited Atonement

John 12:32: [A]nd I, when I am lifted up from the earth, will draw all men to myself.

If Jesus died only for the elect (those who are saved in the end), what does it mean here that all men are drawn to Him? It makes no sense. Those who are "totally depraved" in Reformed/Calvinist thought (the *T* in TULIP) would not be drawn at all. There's no reason to be drawn to Christ in this thinking, since there is no hope whatsoever of being saved, if Christ died only for the elect (limited atonement, or the *L* in TULIP) and not all men.

Moreover, according to the Calvinist notion of irresistible grace (the *I* in TULIP, contra the free will of man) if a man were drawn to Christ, that would already necessarily be grace moving him in that direction (as all Christians agree: God always *starts* the process), and according to Calvinism he wouldn't be able to *resist* it. Yet we know people *do* resist this grace (even accept it and later fall away from or reject it) and are damned.

The passage makes perfect sense, on the other hand, and is coherent within the paradigms of Catholic, Orthodox, and Protestant Arminian/Wesleyan free-will soteriology, but not in

St. John vs. John Calvin on Limited Atonement

Calvinist soteriology. Jesus died for all and offers sufficient grace for anyone to be saved, if he would but accept this free gift of grace. But many reject it.

How does John Calvin interpret the passage? I suspected, before I looked at it, that Calvin would merely play with the word *all* and make out that it doesn't really mean *all*. It doesn't fly. He's unsuccessful. Here's what he wrote, in his *Commentaries*.

> The word "all," which he employs, must be understood to refer to the children of God, who belong to his flock. Yet I agree with Chrysostom, who says that Christ used the universal term, "all," because the Church was to be gathered equally from among Gentiles and Jews.

As usual with Calvin, however (and habitually with anti-Catholics today), he selectively cites the Fathers according to his ends. St. John Chrysostom, of course, believed in universal atonement:

> Now if all have sinned, how come some to be saved, and some to perish? It is because all were not minded to come to Him, since for His part all were saved, for all were called. (Homily XVI on Romans 9:1: v. 9:10; NPNF1-11)

> God, however, being very good, shows the same kindness to both. For it was not those in a state of salvation only to whom He showed mercy, but also Pharaoh, as far as His part went. For of the same long-suffering, both they and he had the advantage. And if he was not saved, it was quite owing to his own will: since, as for what concerneth God, he had as much done for him as they who were saved. (Homily XVI on Romans 9:1: v. 9:22-24; NPNF1-11)

Proving the Catholic Faith Is Biblical

So he says here also, "For the same Lord over all is rich unto all (and upon all)." (Rom. iii. 22.) You see how he sets Him forth as exceedingly desiring our salvation, since He even reckons this to be riches to Himself; so that they are not even now to despair, or fancy that, provided they would repent, they were unpardonable. For He who considereth it as riches to Himself to save us, will not cease to be rich. Since even this is riches, the fact of the gift being shed forth unto all.... "For whosoever," he says, "believeth on Him shall not be ashamed" (Is. xxviii. 16); and, "Whosoever shall call upon the Name of the Lord shall be saved." (Joel ii. 32.) (Homily XVII on Romans 10:1: v. 10:11-13; NPNF1-11)

Ver. 6. "Who gave Himself a ransom for all to be testified in due time." Was Christ then a ransom for the Heathen? Undoubtedly Christ died even for Heathen;... (Homily VII on 1 Timothy, v. 2:6; NPNF1-13)

He came for the salvation of all. (Homily LVII on John, v. 9:8-9; NPNF1-14)

23

God Does Not Predestine the Damned

2 Thessalonians 2:10-11: and with all wicked deception for those who are to perish, because they refused to love the truth and so be saved. Therefore God sends upon them a strong delusion, to make them believe what is false.

They perish (i.e., suffer eternal damnation) "because" they refused to love the truth (the gospel, the revelation of Jesus) that would save them. They had free will and rejected the truth. *Then* God sent them delusion, to believe falsehood. It wasn't God at first who made them believe what is false so they wouldn't be saved. No, *they* chose that, and God accepted their free choice, even though it meant damnation for them.

This takes out the predestination of the damned (standard Calvinist belief), limited atonement, and irresistible grace (a denial of man's ability to reject the grace that God sends), because God's sending the delusion is dependent on the free decisions of men; it's not a decree for all eternity that So-and-so will be damned no matter what he does.

The next verse (2 Thess. 2:12) states: "so that all may be condemned who did not believe the truth but had pleasure in unrighteousness." When they didn't believe the truth, when they still had a chance to be saved, this was their undoing ("because" in that verse).

Then God sent the delusion (v. 11), and the text then reiterates (v. 12) that they are condemned because they refused to believe the truth; *not* because God made it impossible from the outset for them to do so (i.e., predestination of the reprobate, wholly apart from their free choices). They refused it before it was made impossible for them to accept it, by God's decree.

God *does* give *every* person every chance to repent and believe. This is referring to those who are absolutely opposed to God's grace; intransigent, dead-set against God. God knows who will be that way (being omniscient and outside of time, and knowing all things that are still future to us), and so there comes a point where He gives them over to their sin, which is what this passage is talking about (similar to Romans 1:18-27). It is God acknowledging that some men freely reject Him; He honors their free will, but He judges, too.

Nothing here should be troubling at all. It shows that we have free will and that God's grace is always available if we will but accept it and cease our foolish rebellion. "You can lead a horse to water but you can't make it drink." That is like our free will; God won't force us to drink. But His grace and salvation are *there* for us to accept and appropriate in our lives.

24

Prayer, Penance, and the Eternal Destiny of Others

Someone asked me whether a person could theoretically go to hell because others didn't pray for him or didn't pray enough, so that he didn't repent, and noted that this would seem unfair for God to "allow." The questioner was assuming several things here that do not follow.

First, it's not a matter of God's "allowing" someone to go to hell (as if He were to blame for it). If anyone goes to hell, it is because he *wanted* to live without God. As C. S. Lewis wrote with great insight, "The doors of hell are locked on the inside."[6]

Second, all grace, including grace conveyed through prayer, comes from God. Since God knows everything (including even possibilities and contingencies and all possible outcomes), if He foreknew that Person A would not pray for someone else, He could easily "arrange" things in His providence so that Person B would do so.

Third, in the final analysis, whether we are saved will always depend on God's grace, but it is our decision whether to *accept*

---

[6] C. S. Lewis, *The Problem of Pain* (New York: HarperCollins, 2001), 130.

this grace. The grace will be provided. It doesn't *ultimately* depend on another person, so that if *he* fails, *we* go to hell. It just doesn't work that way. That would be contrary to God's mercy, to let eternal salvation rest on the week reed of third parties.

The proper way to express our choice with regard to eternal destiny would be to say (using myself): "Dave did not accept the grace and the free option of going to heaven that God provided for him, and so he went to hell." We all stand before God alone, in the end, as many old folk songs point out, such as: "You got to walk that lonesome valley by yourself."

We mustn't confine ourselves to a merely human way of looking at things. God has a completely different perspective (as revealed in Holy Scripture).

Who is saved and who is damned is not in our hands. We can help provide the avenues of grace and blessing that God has for each individual, but each one's final destiny rests with him and God. We are to pray, do good works, love, do penance on behalf of others, listen, assist, and share the Good News at every reasonable opportunity.

Then we know that we are fulfilling our responsibility and holding up our end of the bargain, so to speak. The good things we do can make the (Christian) path *easier* for others to follow, but they do not *determine* others' paths, let alone whether others go to heaven or hell.

Books such as Proverbs and Psalms present a stark contrast between the "evil, wicked fools" and the "righteous" and the "wise." That's proverbial language, though, which intends to convey generalities. We all know that we are quite the mixture of good and evil and often are more like shades of gray rather than pure and righteous and holy versus utterly evil and wicked. Alexander Solzhenitsyn, the famous Orthodox writer and dissident against Communism stated that "the line between good and evil runs through every human heart."

It is the extreme contrast that is the motivational tool to reform behavior and to express the *urgency* and importance of action on behalf of others. In this matter, there is indeed a relationship between our prayers and graces always caused and offered by God through us to others. The same applies to penitential works and even suffering (redemptive suffering).

God designed things that way, so that we can all be involved in the marvelous process of His graces. He wanted salvation and redemption to be a community or organic effort, not the effort of a bunch of atomistic individuals. We help each other. We are our brothers' keepers.

I think we can, therefore, quite possibly interpret this aspect of the message of Fátima (perhaps in part, at the least) as: "If *no one* prays for a soul, that soul will go to hell." But that is at bottom a *collective* notion: "every soul needs the assistance of prayer [general]; therefore *you* [particular; part of the collective] should pray."

It doesn't logically follow, however, that if we as *individuals* fail to pray for an *individual person*, that person will go to hell, because, as I noted before, God in His Providence will simply cause or urge *another* person to do so.

And even then, a person could receive all kinds of graces through prayer and whatnot, yet still reject God and salvation, because God gave us the free will to do so, so that following Him would be a meaningful choice, not a question of God's pressing a button and our not being able to refuse, as if we were robots.

After all, Satan himself was in heaven with God and had everything he could possibly need or want. But he wanted to be *in God's place*, so it wasn't enough for him. Causation in such matters of final salvation is not strictly a matter of us (i.e., we as individuals) and them.

Or, on a more human level: we have all seen families where two children were raised the same way, yet one rebels and gets into heavy sin, while the other stays faithful to the Church and Christian moral teachings. Free will: both were given the same "graces" so to speak, by the parents, but the outcome was different because *they* decided in the end which way they would go.

The final destiny of the person rests on his acceptance or rejection of God and His grace. We know that God predestines those who will be saved, to salvation, yet (paradoxically) not without their choice and free assent. How this works out in fine detail is a matter of debate in Catholic theology, between Thomists and Molinists. But in Catholic teaching (in contrast to Calvinist), He predestines no one to hell.

25

Biblical Support for Lent

My specialty as an apologist is biblical arguments for Catholicism. I enjoy that aspect of my work a lot because the Bible is the great "common ground" for all Christians (and I strive to be ecumenical). We all reverence Sacred Scripture and believe it is inspired revelation. Along these lines, someone asked me a few years ago on my Facebook page: "How come we celebrate Lent when the word is not in Scripture?"

Trinity (that is, the *word*) is not in Scripture either. Christian church buildings are not in the New Testament at all; it describes Christians as meeting in homes. The term *original sin* is not in the Bible (whereas the concept *is*), nor is the word *theology*.

The Bible never refers explicitly to evangelical "staples" such as the "altar call" or "a personal relationship with Jesus" or "have you accepted Jesus into your heart?" or many other ways of describing things in the Christian life that lots of people probably assume are in there somewhere (sort of like all the ingredients in a tasty vegetable soup).

But the *practices* and *beliefs* regarding Lent (as with these other topics) are, assuredly, eminently biblical. In other words, we can confidently assert (especially when challenged a bit) that if we truly want to be biblical Christians and fully conform our lives to scriptural guidelines and models, Lent (or something similar to it) will be part of our walk with Christ.

Fasting and abstinence, central practices during Lent (*Lent* comes from the Old English word for "spring"), are quite biblical activities. The evidence is extensive—largely from the Old Testament, but also in the New. Here is just a small sampling:

> **Ezra 8:21**: Then I proclaimed a fast there, at the river Ahava, that we might humble ourselves before our God, to seek from him a straight way. (cf. Ezra 8:23; 9:5)
>
> **Nehemiah 9:1**: [T]he people of Israel were assembled with fasting and in sackcloth, and with earth upon their heads. (Ash Wednesday!)
>
> **Psalm 69:10**: I humbled my soul with fasting.
>
> **Luke 2:37**: She did not depart from the temple, worshiping with fasting and prayer night and day.
>
> **Luke 7:33**: For John the Baptist has come eating no bread and drinking no wine; and you say, "He has a demon." (cf. Matt. 11:18; Luke 1:15)
>
> **Acts 13:2-3**: While they were worshiping the Lord and fasting, the Holy Spirit said, "Set apart for me Barnabas and Saul for the work to which I have called them." Then after fasting and praying they laid their hands on them and sent them off.
>
> **Romans 14:3**: Let not him who eats despise him who abstains, and let not him who abstains pass judgment on him who eats; for God has welcomed him.

Biblical Support for Lent

Jesus assumes that fasting will be a regular part of the Christian's life, when He says, "And *when* you fast ..." (Matt. 6:16; repeated in 6:17).

The forty (or so) days of Lenten observance have several parallels in Holy Scripture: Moses' fasts on the holy mountain (Exod. 24:18; 34:28; Deut. 9:9) and his intercession for Israel (Deut. 9:25); Elijah's journey to Mount Horeb (1 Kings 19:8); Ezekiel's lying on one side (Ezek. 4:6); and Christ's fast in the wilderness (Matt. 4:2).

The premise underlying all these practices is *mortification*: the subduing of the body (or, in a similar sense, the "flesh" against the spirit) for spiritual purposes. This is controversial among some, yet it has an explicit biblical basis as well, particularly in this passage from St. Paul:

1 Corinthians 9:27: but I pommel my body and subdue it, lest after preaching to others I myself should be disqualified.

Other Bible versions translate *pommel* as "beat," "bruise," "beating and bruising," "batter," "buffet," "punish," and "discipline." The Goodspeed translation reads: "I beat and bruise my body and make it my slave." Commentators dispute precisely what St. Paul *means*, and the Catholic position does not absolutely require only one interpretation of this passage.

But in any event, even if it is merely metaphorical, it fits into the overall scriptural theme of self-sacrifice, as outlined earlier; therefore, it is expressing a principle or premise regarding some sort of asceticism or what we might call self-discipline, however it is specifically interpreted.

Bottom line: what Catholics and other Christians observe during Lent is altogether in line with biblical teaching. Those

Christians who don't "do" Lent (like me for my first thirty-two years, though I would fast at times) miss out on these important penitential aspects of the Faith and the spiritual blessings and graces obtained therein. What we find in inspired Scripture (especially if it is repeated many times) is important and is intended by God for our spiritual well-being.

26

Divine Chastisement
(or, Purgatory in *This* Life)

I've often used what I call the nutshell argument for purgatory: we must be without sin to enter into God's presence (Eph. 5:5; Heb. 12:14; Rev. 21:27; 22:3, 14-15). Therefore, God must purge or wash away our sin to make us fit to be in heaven with Him. All agree so far.

The only disagreement is whether this "divine cleansing" takes place in an instant or is more of a process. It's merely a quantitative difference, not an essential one. Purgatory is indicated most directly in 1 Corinthians 3:13-15: "[T]he fire will test what sort of work each one has done."

I'd like to examine, however, the notion that this same purging process takes place *before* we die, and not just after — the very common biblical theme of God's chastising or purifying His people.

St. Catherine of Genoa wrote: "How much better is it to be cleansed here than in the other life! For whoever suffers purgation in this life pays but a small portion of what is due, by reason of the liberty of his free-will cooperating with infused grace" (*Spiritual Dialogue*, pt. 2, chap. 2). Her point was that we receive graces and merit during life that are no longer available in purgatory. Therefore, it is preferable to undergo the necessary purification before death rather than after. This is a great and helpful insight for the Christian life, and it's massively supported in the Bible.

Scripture refers to a purging fire: whatever "shall pass through the fire" will be made "clean" (Num. 31:23); "we went through fire" (Ps. 66:12); "our God is a consuming fire" (Heb. 12:29).

The Bible makes frequent use also of the metaphor of various metals being refined (in a fire): "[W]hen he has tried me, I shall come forth as gold" (Job 23:10); "[T]hou, O God, hast tested us; thou hast tried us as silver is tried" (Ps. 66:10); "The crucible is for silver, and the furnace is for gold, and the LORD tries hearts" (Prov. 17:3); "I will turn my hand against you and will smelt away your dross as with lye and remove all your alloy" (Isa. 1:25); "I have refined you.... I have tried you in the furnace of affliction" (Isa. 48:10); "I will refine them and test them" (Jer. 9:7); "I will put this third into the fire, and refine them as one refines silver, and test them as gold is tested" (Zech. 13:9); "[H]e is like a refiner's fire, and like fullers' soap; he will sit as a refiner and purifier of silver, and he will purify the sons of Levi, and refine them like gold and silver" (Mal. 3:2-3); "[Y]our faith, more precious than gold which though perishable is tested by fire" (1 Pet. 1:6-7).

God's cleansing or washing us is another common biblical theme: "Wash me thoroughly from my iniquity, and cleanse me from my sin!... Purge me with hyssop, and I shall be clean" (Ps. 51:2, 7); "Blows that wound cleanse away evil; strokes make clean the innermost parts" (Prov. 20:30); "[T]he Lord shall have washed away the filth of the daughters of Zion and cleansed the bloodstains of Jerusalem from its midst by a spirit of judgment and by a spirit of burning" (Isa. 4:4); "I will cleanse them from

Divine Chastisement

all the guilt of their sin against me" (Jer. 33:8); "I will sprinkle clean water upon you, and you shall be clean from all your uncleannesses" (Ezek. 36:25); "our hearts sprinkled clean from an evil conscience and our bodies washed with pure water" (Heb 10:22); "[H]e was cleansed from his old sins" (2 Pet. 1:9); "[T]he blood of Jesus his Son cleanses us from all sin" (1 John 1:7).

Divine "chastisement" is taught clearly in many passages: "[A]s a man disciplines his son, the LORD your God disciplines you" (Deut. 8:5); "[D]o not despise the LORD's discipline or be weary of his reproof," (Prov. 3:11); "For thou didst test them as a father does in warning" (Wisd. 11:10); "God who tests our hearts" (1 Thess. 2:4); "For the Lord disciplines him whom he loves, and chastises every son whom he receives. It is for discipline that you have to endure. God is treating you as sons; for what son is there whom his father does not discipline? ... [H]e disciplines us for our good, that we may share his holiness" (Heb. 12:6-7, 10).

We are subject to God's indignation or wrath, insofar as we sin: "God will bring every deed into judgment" (Eccles. 12:14); "I will bear the indignation of the Lord because I have sinned against him.... He will bring me forth to the light" (Mic. 7:9).

Purgatory is "written all over" the passages above. I once didn't make the connection of what seems so obvious to me now. I think there are many who (like me) might be persuaded to see that the Bible is far more "Catholic" than they had ever imagined.

27

Mystery Is No Basis for Rejecting Transubstantiation

The first Christian leader of any historical importance to deny the Real Presence in the Eucharist was Huldrych Zwingli (1484-1531), the Swiss Protestant leader. Zwingli wrote:

> And how can we say that it is flesh when we do not perceive it to be such? If the body were there miraculously, the bread would not be bread, but we should perceive it to be flesh. Since, however, we see and perceive bread, it is evident that we are ascribing to God a miracle which he himself neither wills nor approves: for he does not work miracles which cannot be perceived.[7]

The Eucharist was intended by God as a different kind of miracle from the outset, requiring more profound faith, as opposed to the "proof" of tangible, empirical miracles. In this it is certainly not unique among Christian doctrines and traditional beliefs — many fully shared by our Protestant brethren. The

---

[7] Huldrych Zwingli, *On the Lord's Supper*, 1526, translated by G. W. Bromiley.

No Basis for Rejecting Transubstantiation

virgin birth, for example, cannot be observed or proven and is the utter opposite of a *demonstrable* miracle.

Likewise, in the atonement of Jesus the world sees a beaten and tortured man being put to death on a cross. The Christian, on the other hand, sees there the great miracle of redemption and the means of the salvation of mankind—an unspeakably sublime miracle; yet who but those with the eyes of faith can see or believe it?

Baptism, according to most Christians, imparts real, regenerative grace. But this is rarely evident or tangible, especially in infants. Lastly, the Incarnation itself was not able to be perceived as an outward miracle, although it might be considered the most incredible miracle ever. It was not visible or manifest in the outward, concrete way to which Zwingli seems foolishly to think God would or must restrict Himself.

Jesus looked, felt, and sounded like a man; no one but those possessing faith would know (from simply observing Him) that He was also God, an uncreated Person who had made everything in the world on which He stood. No blood test could reveal that.

Jesus stated more than once that seeking outward signs betrays a lack of faith and proper vision: "An evil and adulterous generation seeks for a sign" (Matt. 12:29); "Blessed are those who have not seen and yet believe" (John 20:29). Signs and miracles (that is, in the empirical, sensory way that Zwingli demands for the Eucharist) do not suffice for many hardhearted people in the first place: "If they do not hear Moses and the prophets, neither will they be convinced if some one should rise from the dead" (Luke 16:31).

Does it make sense that Jesus could walk through walls (with a body!) after His Resurrection (John 20:26), but God couldn't or wouldn't have performed the miracle of transubstantiation (literally, "change of substance")? No one should rashly attempt to tie God's hands by such arguments of alleged implausibility. The fact remains that God clearly can perform any miracle, however "strange."

Many Christian beliefs seem unreasonable at first and difficult to grasp with the natural mind and require a great deal of faith. Protestants believe in a number of such doctrines, such as the Trinity, God's eternal existence, omnipotence, the power of prayer, and God's providence. Why should the Real Presence be singled out for excessive skepticism and unchecked rationalism? I contend that it is due to a preconceived bias against sacramentalism, which in a nutshell is matter conveying grace.

This anti-eucharistic bias reminds me of the Jewish and Muslim belief that the Incarnation is unthinkable. They view the Incarnation in the same way as the majority of Protestants regard the Eucharist. For them God wouldn't or couldn't become a man. For evangelicals God wouldn't, couldn't, or shouldn't become substantially, sacramentally present under the outward forms of bread and wine. The dynamic is the same.

If Christ could become Man, He can surely will to become physically present in what continues to appear as bread and wine, once consecrated. The second thing is no less "odd" or possible than the first. Eucharist and Incarnation flow from the same biblically demonstrable premise: God profoundly uses matter for spiritual and redemptive purposes.

I agree with Blessed John Henry Cardinal Newman:

> People say that the doctrine of Transubstantiation is difficult to believe.... It is difficult, impossible to imagine, I grant — but how is it difficult to believe?... For myself, I cannot, indeed prove it, I cannot tell how it is; but I say,

No Basis for Rejecting Transubstantiation

"Why should it not be? What's to hinder it? What do I know of substance or matter? Just as much as the greatest philosophers, and that is nothing at all."[8]

---

[8] John Henry Newman, *Apologia pro vita Sua* (1864), 318, part 7: "General Answer to Mr. Kingsley."

28

On the Nature of Idolatry

Idolatry is a conscious act by nature or definition. Catholics are accused of substituting bread and wine as idols for the living God. I think virtually no Catholic who knows anything at all about his Faith would be stupid enough consciously to worship what he believes is still just a piece of bread.

It may be regarded as *mistaken worship*, but it is still quite pious and nonidolatrous, just as we Catholics would say that Lutheran or Anglican worship is pious and well-intentioned but in fact lacks the Real Presence (due to ordination and apostolic succession issues). It's not idolatrous—only mistaken as to the metaphysics.

Where is the sin in worshipping Jesus Christ our Lord and Savior and Redeemer—God the Son? We think He is truly present in the consecrated elements. So did Luther. If we are idolaters, so is he. Luther was even known to bow in adoration. Lutherans, too, believe that Jesus Christ is truly, substantially present after the Consecration, so why are *they* not habitually accused of idolatry?

It is of the essence of idolatry to be from one's heart and soul and will. If one is replacing God with something else, that is an interior decision. It *has* to be; otherwise, the whole thing would

On the Nature of Idolatry

be reduced to robotic actions of an agent with no free will. This sort of thing is presupposed also in the Sermon on the Mount, where Jesus shows how all sins begin in our hearts: hatred is the seed of murder, lust the kernel of adultery, et cetera. All sin is like that (at least the sin for which we are responsible).

Idolatry is the worshipping of a false god. That does not happen at Mass, because it is understood by all that *Jesus, not bread and wine, is being worshipped* eucharistically. The very word *transubstantiation* proves this. As for its being a matter of the heart and soul: the Bible establishes that, I think:

> **Isaiah 66:3**: like him who blesses an idol. These have chosen their own ways, and *their soul* delights in their abominations.

> **Ezekiel 14:4-5**: Therefore speak to them, and say to them, Thus says the Lord GOD: Any man of the house of Israel who takes his idols *into his heart* and sets the stumbling block of his iniquity before his face, and yet comes to the prophet, I the LORD will answer him myself because of the multitude of his idols, that *I may lay hold of the hearts* of the house of Israel, who are all estranged from me through their idols.

> **Ezekiel 20:16**: because they rejected my ordinances and did not walk in my statutes, and profaned my sabbaths; for *their heart* went after their idols. (cf. Ezek. 36:25; Sir. 46:11)

Another biblical motif is God's disgust over men "serving" idols (which is from the heart and the will: 2 Kings 17:12; 2 Kings 21:21; 2 Chron. 24:18; Ps. 106:36; Ezek. 20:39; 1 Thess. 1:9). St. Paul locates idolatry firmly in the interior disposition:

Proving the Catholic Faith Is Biblical

Romans 1:21, 24-25: [F]or although they knew God they did not honor him as God or give thanks to him, but they became futile in their thinking and their senseless *minds* were darkened.... Therefore God gave them up in the lusts of their *hearts* to impurity, to the dishonoring of their bodies among themselves, because they exchanged the truth about God for a lie and worshiped and served the *creature* rather than the Creator, who is blessed for ever! Amen.

The word for "minds" in Romans 1:21 is *kardia* ("heart": the basis of "cardiac"), and is often rendered "heart" or "hearts" in other translations. The same word appears in Romans 1:24, where it is rendered "hearts" in the RSV. In the KJV it is translated "heart" all 158 times that it appears (according to *Young's Concordance*).

The *Catholic Encyclopedia*'s entry for "Idolatry" backs me up also:

> The guilt of idolatry, however, is not to be estimated by its abstract nature alone; the concrete form it assumes in the *conscience* of the sinner is the *all-important element*.[9]

Idolatry is an internal disposition—the conscious worshipping of something other than God and replacing God with a creature or inanimate object.

---

[9] J. Wilhelm, "Idolatry," *Catholic Encyclopedia*, (New York: Robert Appleton, 1913), http://www.newadvent.org/cathen/07636a.htm.

29

"The Apostle Paul Says He Is a Priest? Where?"

Some Protestants claim that priests are never mentioned in the Bible. Well, in Romans 15:16, Paul says he is a priest. And is this in Catholic versions only? Nope. The following six non-Catholic translations have St. Paul calling himself a "priest" (the Greek word is *hierourgeo* [Strong's word no. 2418]):

> **Moffatt**: as a priest of Christ Jesus to the Gentiles in the service of God's gospel. My aim is to make the Gentiles an acceptable offering, consecrated by the holy Spirit.
>
> **20th Century New Testament**: that I should be a minister of Christ Jesus to go to the Gentiles — that I should act as a priest of God's Good News, so that the offering up of the Gentiles may be an acceptable sacrifice, consecrated by the Holy Spirit.
>
> **Young's Literal Translation**: for my being a servant of Jesus Christ to the nations, acting as priest in the good news of God, that the offering up of the nations may become acceptable, sanctified by the Holy Spirit.
>
> **NASB**: ... ministering as a priest the gospel of God.

Weymouth: that I should be a minister of Christ Jesus among the Gentiles, doing priestly duties in connexion with God's Good News so that the sacrifice—namely the Gentiles—may be acceptable to Him, being (as it is) an offering which the Holy Spirit has made holy.

RSV: to be a minister of Christ Jesus to the Gentiles in the priestly service of the gospel of God, so that the offering of the Gentiles may be acceptable, sanctified by the Holy Spirit.

The NASB is the most interesting because it has a strong evangelical bias, and it *still* uses "priest" because that is clearly what this word means.

Goodspeed also has "priest" and Rotherham Emphasized has "priestly." The NRSV has "priestly service." It looks as if others would likely follow this pattern as well but I didn't look them all up. These eight (not a one, Catholic) are sufficient to establish my point.

The corresponding evidence from lexicons and other similar aids about *hierourgeo* is very strong, too: Kittel (*Theological Dictionary of the New Testament*) says of it: "This term means 'to perform sacred or sacrificial ministry.' In Josephus and Philo it always means 'to offer sacrifice.'" Baptist A. T. Robertson tries to spin it in a Protestant direction but also says, "It means to work in sacred things, to minister as a priest." Marvin Vincent (*Word Studies in the New Testament*) says, "Lit., ministering 'as a priest'." Thayer says: "used esp. of persons sacrificing ... 'to minister in the manner of a priest, minister in priestly service.'"

If anyone tries to claim that priests are never mentioned in the New Testament, this is the passage they need to grapple with.

30

Sacramentalism

God became man. The Incarnation was the event in salvation history that raised matter to previously unknown heights. All created matter was "good" from the start (Gen. 1:25), but was "glorified" by the Incarnation.

Ritual and "physicality" were not abolished by the coming of Christ. Quite the contrary: it was the Incarnation that fully established sacramentalism as a principle in the Christian religion. Sacramentalism may be defined as the belief that matter can convey grace. God uses matter both to help us live better lives (sanctification) and ultimately to save us (regeneration and justification), starting with baptism.

The atonement or redemption by Christ (His death on the Cross for us) was not purely spiritual. It was also as physical (sacramental, if you will) as it could be. Protestants often piously refer to the Blood of Jesus, and rightly so (see, e.g., Rev. 5:9; Eph. 1:7; Col. 1:14; Heb. 9:12; 1 Pet. 1:2; 1 John 1:7). This is explicitly sacramental thinking.

It was the very suffering of Jesus in the flesh, and the voluntary shedding of His blood, that constituted the crucial, essential aspect of His work as our Redeemer and Savior. One can't avoid this: "he was bruised for our iniquities" (Isa. 53:5).

Proving the Catholic Faith Is Biblical

So it is curious that many Protestants appear to possess a pronounced hostility to the sacramental belief of the Real Presence in the Eucharist, seeing that it flows so straightforwardly from the Incarnation and the Crucifixion itself. The New Testament is filled with incarnational and sacramental indications—instances of matter conveying grace. The Church is the Body of Christ (1 Cor. 12:27; Eph. 1:22-23; 5:30), and marriage (including its physical aspects) is described as a direct parallel to Christ and the Church (Eph. 5:22-33, esp. 29-32). Jesus even equates Himself in some sense with the Church, saying He was "persecuted" by Paul after the Resurrection (Acts 9:5).

Not only that, but in St. Paul's teaching, one can find a repeated theme of identifying very graphically and literally with Christ and His sufferings (see 2 Cor. 4:10; Phil. 2:17; 3:10; 2 Tim. 4:6; and above all, Col. 1:24).

Matter conveys grace all over the place in Scripture: baptism confers regeneration (Acts 2:38; 22:16; 1 Pet. 3:21; cf. Mark 16:16; Rom. 6:3-4; 1 Cor. 6:11; Titus 3:5). Paul's "handkerchiefs" healed the sick (Acts 19:12), as did Peter's shadow (Acts 5:15), Jesus' garment (Matt. 9:20-22) and His saliva mixed with dirt (John 9:5ff.; Mark 8:22-25), and water from the pool of Siloam (John 9:7).

Anointing with oil for healing is encouraged (James 5:14). We also observe in Scripture the laying on of hands for the purpose of ordination and commissioning (Acts 6:6; 1 Tim. 4:14; 2 Tim. 1:6) to facilitate the initial outpouring of the Holy Spirit (Acts 8:17-19; 13:3; 19:6), and for healing (Mark 6:5; Luke 13:13; Acts 9:17-18).

Even under the old covenant, a dead man was raised simply by coming in contact with the bones of the prophet Elisha (2 Kings 13:21), which is also one of the direct evidences for the

Sacramentalism

Catholic practice of the veneration of relics (itself an extension of the sacramental principle).

Sacramentalism is a "product" of the Incarnation, as the Church is. But we must also understand that the sacraments are not "magic charms." The Church also teaches that one should have the correct interior disposition when receiving them. The great catechist Fr. John A. Hardon, S.J., wrote, in an entry on "Sacramental Dispositions":

> Condition of soul required for the valid and/or fruitful reception of the sacraments.... In the recipient who has the use of reason is required merely that no obstacles be placed in the way. Such obstacles are a lack of faith or sanctifying grace or of a right intention.[10]

Likewise, the *Catechism of the Catholic Church*, in its section on *ex opere operato* (no. 1128), notes: "Nevertheless, the fruits of the sacraments also depend on the disposition of the one who receives them."

The sacrament of the Eucharist, for example, will not have a positive effect or convey grace if received by a person in mortal sin (see 1 Cor. 11:27-30; CCC 1415), and priestly absolution is null and void without the necessary prerequisite of true repentance.

This is all the more true of sacramentals (such as holy water, scapulars, blessings, the Miraculous Medal, genuflection, et cetera), which depend entirely on the inner state of the one using or receiving them. Intent, sincerity, motivation, piety, and suchlike are all supremely important in the Catholic life. A person who

---

[10]*Modern Catholic Dictionary* (Garden City, New York: Doubleday, 1980), 477.

wears a scapular but neglects the pursuit of righteousness and obedience and views the scapular as a magic charm (which is occultic superstition) will not receive the benefits of the sacramental. A piece of cloth cannot rescind the normal duties of the Catholic life. Nor is God some sort of celestial vending machine. He wants our *hearts*; he wants *us* — not meaningless outward obedience without the proper interior motivation, in love, and by His grace. Sacraments help us, but we must do our part, too.

31

Ritualistic and Formal Worship

All Christians are tempted at times merely to go through the motions of Christianity, lacking passion and commitment and wholehearted devotion. This charge seems often to be directed at Catholics in terms of how we worship. It's said that the Mass is too "ritualistic" and that this leads to rote observance without wholehearted participation.

Does the Bible teach that formal worship is inevitably or even usually "cold" and "dead" (as critics would have it)? If formal worship or religious ritual were always and intrinsically opposed to sincere, heartfelt adoration and praise of God, then certainly God wouldn't have commanded it in the Bible. Yet we find that He does exactly that, in many places.

It is abundantly clear in the Old Testament. Elaborate, painstaking instructions for the ark of the covenant (Exod. 25:1-22), the tabernacle (Exod. 25:23-40; 26-27), and the Temple (1 Kings 6-7) illustrate the highly ritualistic nature of Hebrew worship (see also Lev. 23:37-38; 24.5-8).

Formal and ritualistic ceremonies and worship services are recorded as taking place even in heaven itself:

Revelation 4:8-11: And the four living creatures, each of them with six wings, are full of eyes all round and within, and day and night they never cease to sing, "Holy, holy, holy, is the Lord God Almighty, who was and is and is to come!" And whenever the living creatures give glory and honor and thanks to him who is seated on the throne, who lives for ever and ever, the twenty-four elders fall down before him who is seated on the throne and worship him who lives for ever and ever; they cast their crowns before the throne, singing, "Worthy art thou, our Lord and God, to receive glory and honor and power, for thou didst create all things, and by thy will they existed and were created."

Revelation 5:6-14: And between the throne and the four living creatures and among the elders, I saw a Lamb standing, as though it had been slain, with seven horns and with seven eyes, which are the seven spirits of God sent out into all the earth; and he went and took the scroll from the right hand of him who was seated on the throne. And when he had taken the scroll, the four living creatures and the twenty-four elders fell down before the Lamb, each holding a harp, and with golden bowls full of incense, which are the prayers of the saints; and they sang a new song, saying, "Worthy art thou to take the scroll and to open its seals, for thou wast slain and by thy blood didst ransom men for God from every tribe and tongue and people and nation, and hast made them a kingdom and priests to our God, and they shall reign on earth." Then I looked, and I heard around the throne and the living creatures and the elders the voice of many angels, numbering myriads of myriads and thousands of thousands, saying with a loud voice, "Worthy is the Lamb who was

Ritualistic and Formal Worship

slain, to receive power and wealth and wisdom and might and honor and glory and blessing!" And I heard every creature in heaven and on earth and under the earth and in the sea, and all therein, saying, "To him who sits upon the throne and to the Lamb be blessing and honor and glory and might for ever and ever!" And the four living creatures said, "Amen!" and the elders fell down and worshiped

With "thousands of thousands" and "every creature in heaven and on earth" all uttering the same praise or prayer (or liturgy, if you will) at the same time, it's obvious that these are form prayers and formal worship: distinguishable from (sincere) spontaneous praise and worship (with its *praise the Lord*s and *Hallelujah*s and *Glory to God*s).

Note that these examples include repetitious prayer (Rev. 4:8: "they never cease to sing"), repeated chants or hymns (Rev. 4:11; 5:9-10), and sacrifice (Rev. 5:6). Revelation 8:3-4 also mentions an altar and incense. It seems quite clear, then, that the Bible is not opposed to ritual or to formality (in either worship or prayer) at all. What God *does* oppose is *hypocritical* worship, lacking the proper attitude of heart toward God. This is an ongoing human tendency that we all must be vigilant (by His grace) to avoid:

Amos 5:12, 21-22: For I know how many are your transgressions, and how great are your sins.... I hate, I despise your feasts, and I take no delight in your solemn assemblies. Even though you offer me your burnt offerings and cereal offerings, I will not accept them. (cf. Prov. 15:8; Jer. 6:19-20)

Matthew 5:23-24: So if you are offering your gift at the altar, and there remember that your brother has something against you, leave your gift there before the altar and go; first be reconciled to your brother, and then come and offer your gift.

Matthew 6:1-2: Beware of practicing your piety before men in order to be seen by them; for then you will have no reward from your Father who is in heaven. Thus, when you give alms, sound no trumpet before you, as the hypocrites do in the synagogues and in the streets, that they may be praised by men. (cf. Matt. 6:3-6, 16; 23:23-28)

Matthew 15:7-9: You hypocrites! Well did Isaiah prophesy of you, when he said: "This people honors me with their lips, but their heart is far from me; in vain do they worship me, teaching as doctrines the precepts of men."

What God opposes is deceit and spiritual hypocrisy, and worship (whether formal or informal) devoid of a committed, heartfelt spirit and devotion, or in conjunction with continued sin and disobedience.

32

Is the Rosary "Vain Repetition"?

A new Catholic convert who was struggling with some things in the Faith asked me about the Rosary some years ago: "Mary is most often mentioned in the Rosary. I find it difficult meditating on Christ when Mary is so prevalent. Why is Mary so heavily infused into the prayer?"

Here is my reply:

One must understand the nature of the Rosary and the purpose of the repetition. Most of the words of the Hail Mary are, it should be noted, straight from the Bible. And it's incorrect to say that because *Mary* might be the word repeated more than any other in the Rosary, that therefore she is considered more important than Jesus or is the focus of the Rosary meditation. The intent of the repetitions of the Hail Mary is to form a sort of background music, so to speak, to the meditations on (mostly) the life of Jesus.

It reminds me of an analogy from my days as a trombone player in my high school band and orchestra. At graduations every year, we had to play the famous *Pomp and Circumstance*, by Edward Elgar. Now, was the purpose of the commencement ceremony to hear *Pomp and Circumstance* seventy-one times? No, of course not. It was to honor the graduates for their accomplishment in achieving a high school diploma. The music was the *background*, just as a soundtrack to a movie is.

It's not a perfect analogy (few are), but the Hail Marys in the Rosary are, at least in part, a sort of rhythmic background to the meditations. The repetition offers a way (rather ingenious, when fully understood) to move forward in the prayer and to avoid distraction (something we are all very familiar with when we try to pray).

You say it is difficult to meditate on Christ while repeating the Hail Mary. This is, I would venture to guess, probably mostly a function of the unfamiliarity with the Rosary. It's very different from much of Protestant piety, just as things such as penance and purgatory and prayers for the dead or asking saints to pray for us are quite foreign at first to the typical Protestant mind. It's a "learned art," to a large extent. Your experience is common to many converts.

We find in the Bible a similar sort of repetitious, chantlike form. Take, for example, Psalm 136, in which the same phrase: "for his steadfast love endures forever" is repeated for twenty-six straight verses! The Hail Marys in the Rosary are somewhat like that. But they are not "vain repetitions" (Matt. 6:7, KJV; cf. "heap up empty phrases," RSV; also Sir. 7:14: "Do not ... repeat yourself in your prayer").

Protestants who argue that all formal prayers that repeat phrases are "empty" or "vain" overlook the entire deeper meaning and import of this biblical narrative in context. Jesus is recommending and exhorting His hearers to a *genuine, humble piety of the heart*, as opposed to an empty, shell-like, merely external piety, intended to be seen by others in a spiritually prideful sense.

This theme of authentic versus sham piety is prevalent in the Sermon on the Mount (see Matt. 6:1-6, 16; cf. Matt. 7:20-23;

Is the Rosary "Vain Repetition"?

15:9). The same general idea is also observed in Mark (12:38-40) and Luke (20:46-47). It's not that all long prayers are condemned, any more than repetitious prayers are, but that prayers made with a pretentious, prideful spirit (showing off in front of others; trying to make people think one is "superpious") are condemned.

Lastly, in Matthew 6:7, Jesus qualifies what He is opposing in prayer, with, "as the Gentiles do." He's not talking about the Hebrew tradition of prayer (which quite obviously included much repetition, such as in the psalms and priestly chants and prayers). He's not even talking about (His frequent target) the Pharisees, but rather the "pagan" or "heathen" (according to various translations) Romans and Greeks: people who followed a different and ultimately false religion. That element and the aspect of interior piety indicate that the passage is far more than merely a discussion of repetition: let alone *all* repetition, as if God is condemning *that*.

Jesus Himself used repetition in prayer. For example: "he went away and prayed for the third time, saying the same words" (Matt. 26:44; cf. Mark 14:39). Moreover, we know that worship in heaven is *extremely* repetitious:

> **Revelation 4:8**: [D]ay and night they never cease to sing, "Holy, holy, holy, is the Lord God Almighty, who was and is and is to come!"

We should recall all these things the next time we hear repetitious or indeed any *formal* prayer condemned as "vain repetition" or supposedly impious by nature. Citing one scriptural passage out of context without considering related biblical data is always dangerous.

33

Asking Saints to Intercede Is a Teaching of Jesus

Have you ever talked to anyone who said: "The Bible never shows anyone praying to anyone other than God! And we can never communicate to anyone who is dead, either. That's occultic!" Yet it's indisputable that Jesus indeed plainly teaches the very thing that they claim is nonexistent in Scripture. In His story of Lazarus and the rich man (Luke 16:19-31), we find our compelling prooftext:

> **Luke 16:24**: And he called out, "Father Abraham, have mercy upon me, and send Lazarus to dip the end of his finger in water and cool my tongue; for I am in anguish in this flame."

This is the Abraham of the Bible—long dead by that time—being asked to do something by a "rich man" (Luke 16:19, 22), traditionally known as Dives (a Latin word for "rich man"). Abraham's answer was, in effect, no (Luke 16:25-26). Having failed in that request, Dives prays to him again for something else:

> **Luke 16:27-28**: And he said, "Then I beg you, father [KJV: "I pray thee therefore, father"], to send him to my

Asking Saints to Intercede

father's house, for I have five brothers, so that he may warn them, lest they also come into this place of torment."

His request is again declined. He argues with Abraham, but Abraham reiterates that what he asks is futile (Luke 16:29-31). All of this reveals to us that not only can dead saints hear our requests; they also have some measure of power to *carry them out on their own* (although no doubt by God's power). Abraham is asked to "send" a dead man to appear to the rich man's brothers, so that they might avoid damnation.

Abraham doesn't deny that he is *able* to send Lazarus to do such a thing; he only denies that it would *work* (by the logic of "if they don't respond to greater factor *x*, they will not respond to lesser factor *y*"). Therefore, it is assumed in the story that Abraham had the ability and authority to do so on his own. And this is all taught, remember, by our Lord Jesus.

The fact that Dives is dead (in the story they are both in *Hades* or *Sheol*: the intermediate netherworld) is irrelevant to the argument at hand, since standard Protestant theology holds that no one should make such a request to anyone but God. Dives asks Abraham to send Lazarus to him, and then to his brothers, so that they can avoid his fate.

That is very much a prayer: asking for supernatural aid from those who have left the earthly life and attained a greater perfection. Also, rather strikingly (and disturbingly for Protestant theology), God is never mentioned in the entire story of Lazarus and the rich man. It's all about Dives asking or praying to Abraham for two requests.

Protestant theology also generally teaches that we can't talk to anyone who is dead, let alone make intercessory requests to them. Yet King Saul talked to the dead prophet Samuel (1 Sam.

28:12-15), Moses and Elijah appeared at the Mount of Transfiguration (Matt. 17:1-3), the "two witnesses" of Revelation (11:3-13) came back to life again (and talked to folks); so did those who rose after Jesus' Resurrection (Matt. 27:50-53).

One reply is to maintain that "this is only a *parable*"; therefore we are told that it doesn't "prove" anything. But many Bible commentators agree that it's *not* a parable. Parables don't use proper names: let alone that of a familiar historical figure such as Abraham. Parables are also prefaced by a statement (usually by the Bible writer, not Jesus) that the words following are to be considered a parable. Nor do I recall any other parables referring to Hades. They are in almost all instances quite "earthy" illustrations: often using agricultural and master and servant word pictures.

But even if we grant for the sake of argument that it *is* a parable, the difficulties for Protestants are not overcome at all, since even parables cannot contain things that are theologically false, lest Jesus be guilty of leading people into heresy by means of untrue illustrations or analogies.

In fact, my contention would be even *stronger* if it is a parable, for in a nonparable, a person could do or say something theologically incorrect. But in a parable taught by Jesus, who is God and is omniscient, in an inspired, infallible revelation, falsehood could not be "enshrined." What Jesus is teaching His hearers cannot contain theological error, and arguments by analogy (basically what parables are) cannot contain false principles.

We conclude, then, that Jesus sanctioned praying to dead men for requests. That is the traditional notion of the Communion of Saints.

34

Praying to Angels and Angelic Intercession

Non-Catholic Christians believe that we can pray to no one but God and ask no one to fulfill an intercessory prayer request but God. But what does the Bible teach?

In the Old Testament, Lot makes such a request of two angels, who were sent by God to destroy Sodom and Gomorrah (Gen. 19:13):

> **Genesis 19:20**: "Behold, yonder city is near enough to flee to, and it is a little one. Let me escape there ... and my life will be saved!"

One of them grants his "prayer": "Behold, I grant you this favor also, that I will not overthrow the city of which you have spoken" (Gen. 19:21). Someone might say, "But the angel wasn't in heaven." Location makes no difference: the angel still fulfilled an intercessory request.

Angels can talk to us from heaven. For example: "[T]he angel of God called to Hagar from heaven" (Gen. 21:17). And we know that angels pray to God for us; such as the "angel of the Lord" praying to God for the inhabitants of Jerusalem and other cities of Judah (Zech. 1:12), and the angel offering to God at the altar in heaven the "prayers of the saints" (Rev. 8:3-4).

Proving the Catholic Faith Is Biblical

When Jacob wrestled with the angel (Gen. 32:24-29), he asked the angel to bless him, and the angel did so (Gen. 32:28-29). Moreover, when Jacob (Israel) blessed his sons Joseph and Manasseh, he asked not only God to bless them, but also an angel ("the angel who has redeemed me from all evil, bless the lads": Gen. 48:16).

One common response to arguments like this is to note that the "angel of the Lord" is actually God Himself, or Jesus in a sort of pre-incarnate manifestation or "theophany": as suggested by many passages (Gen. 22:10-18; 31:11-13; Exod. 3:2-6, 14-16 [Moses and the burning bush]; 13:21; cf. 14:19; Judges 2:1; 6:12-14; Josh. 5:14-15; Zech. 12:8; Acts 8:26, 29). This is a quite respectable harmonization of the scriptural data: held, in fact, by many Eastern Church Fathers.

Yet in other passages "the angel of the Lord" is distinguished from God (Zech. 1:12 and the following):

> **2 Samuel 24:16**: And when the angel stretched forth his hand toward Jerusalem to destroy it, the LORD repented of the evil, and said to the angel who was working destruction among the people, "It is enough; now stay your hand." And the angel of the LORD was by the threshing floor of Araunah the Jebusite.

This ambiguity (seeming equation with God in many places, and distinction from Him in others) is explained by St. Augustine, as cited in the 1911 *Catholic Encyclopedia* article on "Angels":

> St. Augustine (*Sermo* vii, *de Scripturis*, PG V) when treating of the burning bush (Exodus 3) ... points out: "Elsewhere in the Bible when a prophet speaks it is yet said to

Praying to Angels and Angelic Intercession

be the Lord who speaks, not of course because the prophet is the Lord but because the Lord is in the prophet; and so in the same way when the Lord condescends to speak through the mouth of a prophet or an angel, it is the same as when he speaks by a prophet or apostle, and the angel is correctly termed an angel if we consider him himself, but equally correctly is he termed 'the Lord' because God dwells in him.... It is the name of the indweller, not of the temple."

Scripture also clarifies how the angel of the Lord is a unique representative of God:

Exodus 23:20-22: "Behold, *I send an angel* before you, to guard you on the way and to bring you to the place which I have prepared. Give heed to him and hearken to his voice, do not rebel against him, for *he will not pardon your transgression*; for *my name is in him*. But if you hearken attentively to his voice and do all that I say, then I will be an enemy to your enemies and an adversary to your adversaries. When *my angel* goes before you." (cf. Exod. 33:14)

The angel being delegated to pardon transgressions is an interesting precursor to priestly absolution and "binding and loosing."

Therefore, given these Scripture passages and analysis we may also, I submit, plausibly interpret the "angel of the Lord" as a created angel who nevertheless profoundly "carries" God's name and presence.

Such intermediaries between men and God should not surprise us, since even the Law was mediated to men by angels: "delivered" by them (Acts 7:53), "ordained by angels through an intermediary" (Gal. 3:19), and "declared by angels" (Heb. 2:2). Angels even help distribute His grace (Rev. 1:4). Thus, as we have already seen in the Bible: angels can be prayed to and answer prayers, as an additional mediatorial angelic function.

35

Worshipping God through Images in Scripture

Exodus 33:9-11: When Moses entered the tent, the pillar of cloud would descend and stand at the door of the tent, and the LORD would speak with Moses. And when all the people saw the pillar of cloud standing at the door of the tent, all the people would rise up and worship, every man at his tent door. Thus the LORD used to speak to Moses face to face, as a man speaks to his friend.

2 Chronicles 7:1-4: When Solomon had ended his prayer, fire came down from heaven and consumed the burnt offering and the sacrifices, and the glory of the LORD filled the temple. And the priests could not enter the house of the LORD, because the glory of the LORD filled the LORD's house. When all the children of Israel saw the fire come down and the glory of the LORD upon the temple, they bowed down with their faces to the earth on the pavement, and worshiped and gave thanks to the LORD, saying, "For he is good, for his steadfast love endures for ever." Then the king and all the people offered sacrifice before the LORD.

According to Reformed Protestant iconoclastic thinking, these people were worshipping a cloud and fire. I say they were worshipping God *through* those images. If not, then the Bible wouldn't have presented these things positively. They would have been condemned as idolatry. But they were not.

Idolatry (biblically defined) is a matter of the heart. It isn't just a matter of plaster and wood. Idolatry entails substituting any created thing for God Himself. Using something as a visual or devotional aid is not *necessarily* or always doing that. One is worshipping God by means of the visual aid.

In order for praying before a crucifix, for example, to be idolatry (as some Protestants hold) the person praying would have to believe that the image on the crucifix is (1) actually God, or a god and (2) meant to replace the one true God as a substitute (an idol). I submit that virtually no Christian in the history of the world who knows *anything* about the Faith has ever done such a silly thing. They're obviously worshipping Jesus (God) by means of the visual aid.

I can see how a Protestant would object to a statue of Mary or another saint, because they falsely think veneration is worship, and worship belongs only to God. But I can't understand (even under Protestant premises) the objection to a statue of Jesus or a crucifix: not since the Incarnation, in which Jesus became the "image [Greek, *eikon*] of the invisible God."

Protestants have no objection, oddly enough, to statues of Luther in front of seminaries, or huge statues of John Calvin and three other guys in Geneva on the "Reformation Wall."

The Ten Commandments don't forbid all images, but only "graven images," which were specifically intended to be gods to be worshipped. God had represented Himself visually in all kinds of ways: the burning bush, the pillar of cloud, theophanies, the angel of the Lord, and finally Jesus Himself, who *is* God, and quite visual.

36

Martin Luther and the Intercession of the Saints

In the introduction to Martin Luther's commentary on the Magnificat,[11] translator Albert T. W. Steinhaeuser wrote:

> Although Luther regards her [Mary] in one place as sinless, and invokes her aid and intercession at the beginning and close of his work, these are isolated instances; the whole tenor of the exposition is evangelical, and as far removed from the Mariolatry of Rome as from an ultra-protestant depreciation of the Mother of our Lord. (p. 120)

The Blessed Virgin Mary is described by Luther as sinless (my italics):

> Mary also freely ascribes all to God's grace, not to her merit. For *though she was without sin*, yet that grace was too surpassing great for her to deserve it in any way. How

---

[11] Martin Luther, *Works of Martin Luther*, trans. Albert T. W. Steinhaeuser, vol. 3 (Grand Rapids, MI: Baker Book House, 1982), 123-200.

should a creature deserve to become the Mother of God! (p. 161)

In the introduction three places are noted where Luther asked for or mentioned Mary's invocation or intercession (my italics again):

> May the tender Mother of God herself *procure for me* the spirit of wisdom, profitably and thoroughly to expound this song of hers, so that your Grace as well as we all may draw therefrom wholesome knowledge and a praiseworthy life, and thus come to chant and sing this Magnificat eternally in heaven. (p. 125)
>
> That is why I said Mary does not desire to be an idol; she does nothing, God does all. *We ought to call upon her, that for her sake God may grant and do what we request. Thus also all other saints are to be invoked*, so that the work may be every way God's alone. (p. 164)

Very Catholic! Luther understands biblical paradox: God does all; at the same time (without contradiction) He uses *us* to do it.

> We pray God to give us a right understanding of this Magnificat, an understanding that consists not merely in brilliant words, but in glowing life in body and soul. *May Christ grant us this through the intercession and for the sake of His dear Mother Mary.* Amen. (p. 198)

Therefore, Luther at this time believed in the invocation and intercession of the saints, including Mary. This writing (so says Steinhaeuser) was completed by June 10, 1521, and published in late August or early September 1521.

Martin Luther and the Intercession of the Saints

Later, Luther changed his view on those things, but he still believed them as late as *after* the famous Diet of Worms ("Here I stand!"), which ran from January 28 to May 25, 1521.

37

The False Doctrine of "Soul Sleep"

Matthew 27:52, 1 Corinthians 15:20, and 1 Thessalonians 4:13-15 are instances of what is called "phenomenological" language: the language of outward description or appearance rather than complete metaphysical analysis. To us the dead appear to be "asleep."

Jesus Himself used this sort of language, when He described the daughter of Jairus, who had died: "Do not weep, for she is not dead, but sleeping" (Luke 8:52). Then He said, "Child arise" "and her spirit returned" (Luke 8:54-55), thus proving that it was *separate* from her body. Consciousness after death is clearly taught in Scripture:

> **Matthew 10:28**: And do not fear those who kill the body but cannot kill the soul; rather fear him who can destroy both soul and body in hell.
>
> **Revelation 6:9-10**: When he opened the fifth seal, I saw under the altar the souls of those who had been slain for the word of God and for the witness they had borne; they cried out with a loud voice, "O Sovereign Lord, holy and true, how long before thou wilt judge and avenge our blood on those who dwell upon the earth?"

The False Doctrine of "Soul Sleep"

> **1 Kings 17:21-22**: Then he stretched himself upon the child three times, and cried to the LORD, "O LORD my God, let this child's soul come into him again." And the LORD hearkened to the voice of Elijah; and the soul of the child came into him again, and he revived. (cf. Luke 8:53-55)

In the above passages, the soul is described as a separate entity from the body.

> **Psalm 116:15**: Precious in the sight of the LORD is the death of his saints.

The consciousness of the dead is assumed here, or else this verse becomes ludicrous.

Jehovah's Witnesses, Seventh-Day Adventists, and other sects that teach what is known as *annihilationism* or *soul-sleep* (no consciousness after death and no hell, with the sinner being annihilated out of existence altogether), typically rely on the distortion of a few passages in order to "prove" their error:

> **Ecclesiastes 9:5**: [T]he dead know nothing, and they have no more reward.

If the first clause is understood in an absolute sense, then so must the second clause be interpreted. Thus, the dead would have no "reward" as well as no consciousness. This would deny the resurrection and the rewarding of the righteous (see Rev. 20:11-13; 21:6-7; 22:12, 14). Obviously, then, a qualification of some sort has to be placed on Ecclesiastes 9:5.

In the very next verse, we learn that "they have no more for ever any share in all that is done under the sun." In other words, in relation to *this* world, the dead know nothing, but they are in a *different realm*, where they *do* know something. As further examples of this limited sense of "not knowing anything" in Scripture, see 1 Samuel 20:39 and 2 Samuel 15:11, where an interpretation of unconsciousness would be ridiculous.

Ezekiel 18:4: Behold, all souls are mine; the soul of the father as well as the soul of the son is mine: the soul that sins shall die. (cf. Ezek. 18:20)

Here, the *spiritual* use of *death* in the Bible is overlooked. For instance, 1 Timothy 5:6 reads: "[S]he who is self-indulgent is dead even while she lives" (cf. Eph. 2:1 and Luke 15:24). That Ezekiel 18:4, 20 refer to *spiritual death* (i.e., *separation* from God, not annihilation) is obvious from context, since Ezekiel 18:21 declares:

But if a wicked man turns away from all his sins which he has committed and keeps all my statutes and does what is lawful and right, he shall surely live; he shall not die.

Since all men die physically, this must be talking about the spiritual, or "second" death. So much for this "proof" of soul sleep or annihilationism.

Psalm 146:4: When his breath departs he returns to his earth; on that very day his plans perish.

This verse's meaning is similar to that of Ecclesiastes 9:5. Here, "plans" ["thoughts" in KJV] refer to unaccomplished purposes of a person on earth. Death puts an end to those purposes, as anyone would agree. In this sense, one's thoughts or plans "perish" at death. Another similar use occurs at Isaiah 55:7: "[L]et the wicked forsake his way, and the unrighteous man his thoughts." It doesn't mean that unrighteous men must cease all thinking

The False Doctrine of "Soul Sleep"

and become unconscious and nonexistent. Nor does Psalm 146:4.

Much of this sort of inadequate and erroneous exegesis results from a profound lack of understanding of the many literary forms and devices used in Scripture, as seen in these three examples. Much of the Old Testament is poetry of one sort or another. One cannot interpret poetry in a wooden, literal way.

38

Veneration of Saints

Romans 15:18: For I will not venture to speak of anything except what Christ has wrought through me to win obedience from the Gentiles, by word and deed.

1 Corinthians 3:5: What then is Apollos? What is Paul? Servants through whom you believed, as the Lord assigned to each.

2 Corinthians 2:14: But thanks be to God, who in Christ always leads us in triumph, and through us spreads the fragrance of the knowledge of him everywhere.

2 Corinthians 5:20: So we are ambassadors for Christ, God making his appeal through us. We beseech you on behalf of Christ, be reconciled to God.

2 Corinthians 11:10: As the truth of Christ is in me, this boast of mine shall not be silenced in the regions of Achaia.

2 Corinthians 13:3: Christ is speaking in me.

Galatians 2:8: [F]or he who worked through Peter for the mission to the circumcised worked through me also for the Gentiles.

Veneration of Saints

Galatians 2:20: I have been crucified with Christ; it is no longer I who live, but Christ who lives in me; and the life I now live in the flesh I live by faith in the Son of God, who loved me and gave himself for me.

Philippians 1:26: so that in me you may have ample cause to glory in Christ Jesus, because of my coming to you again.

Philippians 4:9: What you have learned and received and heard and seen in me, do; and the God of peace will be with you.

1 Timothy 1:16: [B]ut I received mercy for this reason, that in me, as the foremost, Jesus Christ might display his perfect patience for an example to those who were to believe in him for eternal life.

Titus 1:3: and at the proper time manifested in his word through the preaching with which I have been entrusted by command of God our Savior.

If St. Paul is saying that all of these things "in" or "through" him were because of Christ and that others see these things "in" or "through" him, does it not follow that Paul could be venerated, precisely because of what was "in" or "through" him and was observed by others, to their edification? The Catholic doctrine of veneration, after all, means honoring a creature because he profoundly reflects the grace and love and other attributes of God.

Although this is merely a deductive proof to some extent, I think it works on some level, especially because elsewhere, many times, Paul urges his followers to "imitate" him, as he in turn imitated Jesus Christ.

39

The Perpetual Virginity of Mary

Once upon a time, virtually no Christians—including Protestants—denied that Mary the Mother of Jesus was perpetually a virgin. Of the early leaders of the Protestant movement, including Luther, Calvin, Zwingli, Bullinger, and Cranmer, virtually all fully accepted this doctrine. Moreover, most Protestant exegetes *continued* to believe it for at least another 350 years or so.

But today (for various reasons) things are very different, so it's helpful to revisit the biblical arguments, since the Bible is the authority all Christians revere. A surprising number can be found:

1. Luke 2:41-51 describes Mary and Joseph taking Jesus to the Temple at the age of twelve, for the required observance of Passover. Everyone agrees that He was the first child of Mary, so if there were up to five or more siblings, as some maintain (or even one), why is there no hint of them at all in this account?

2. Neither Hebrew nor Aramaic has a word for *cousin*. The New Testament was written in Greek, which does have such a word (*sungenis*), but Jesus and His disciples spoke Aramaic (a late version of Hebrew), and the Hebrew word *ach* is literally translated as *adelphos,* the literal equivalent of the English *brother*. In the

The Perpetual Virginity of Mary

Bible, it has a very wide range of meanings beyond "sibling," just as *brother* does in English. Thus, it is routinely used in the New Testament to describe cousins or kinsmen, et cetera.

3. Jesus Himself uses *brethren* (*adelphos*) in a nonsibling sense. In Matthew 23:8 (cf. Matt. 12:49-50), He calls, for example, the "crowds" and His "disciples" (23:1) "brethren." In other words, they are *each other's* "brothers": the brotherhood of Christians.

4. In comparing Matthew 27:56, Mark 15:40, and John 19:25, we find that James and Joseph (mentioned in Matthew 13:55 with Simon and Jude as Jesus' "brothers") are the sons of Mary, the wife of Clopas. This other Mary (Matt. 27:61; 28:1) is called our Lady's *adelphe* in John 19:25. Assuming that there are not two women named Mary in one family, this usage apparently refers to a cousin or a more distant relative. Matthew 13:55-56 and Mark 6:3 mention Simon, Jude, and "sisters" along with James and Joseph, calling all *adelphoi*. The most plausible interpretation of all this related data is a use of *adelphos* as "cousins" (or possibly, stepbrothers) rather than "siblings." We know for sure, from the above information, that James and Joseph were not Jesus' siblings.

It's not mere special pleading to argue in this fashion (as is charged), or an alleged desperation of Catholics who supposedly "read into" the texts their prior belief in the dogma of perpetual virginity. Plenty of Protestant exegesis and scholarship confirms these views: especially in older commentaries. For example, the prominent nineteenth-century *Commentary on the Whole Bible*, by Jamieson, Fausset, and Brown, states, regarding Matthew 13:55 (my italics added):

> An *exceedingly difficult question* here arises—What were these "brethren" and "sisters" to Jesus? Were they, First,

Proving the Catholic Faith Is Biblical

His full brothers and sisters? or, Secondly, Were they His *step-brothers and step-sisters*, children of Joseph by a former marriage? or, Thirdly, Were they His *cousins, according to a common way of speaking among the Jews* respecting persons of collateral descent? On this subject an immense deal has been written, nor are opinions yet by any means agreed.... In addition to other objections, *many of the best interpreters ... prefer the third opinion....* Thus dubiously we prefer to leave this *vexed question, encompassed as it is with difficulties.*

5. The Blessed Virgin Mary is committed to the care of the apostle John by Jesus from the Cross (John 19:26-27). Jesus certainly wouldn't have done this if He had brothers (all of whom would have been younger than He was).

6. Matthew 1:24-25 says, "Joseph ... knew her not *until* she had borne a son." This passage has been used as an argument that Mary did not remain a virgin after the birth of Jesus, but the same Protestant commentary also states (my italics again):

The word "till" [*until* above] does not necessarily imply that they lived on a different footing afterwards (as will be evident from the use of the same word in 1 Samuel 15:35; 2 Samuel 6:23; Matthew 12:20); nor does the word "firstborn" decide the *much-disputed question*, whether Mary had any children to Joseph after the birth of Christ; for, as Lightfoot says, "The law, in speaking of the first-born, regarded not whether any were born *after* or no, but only that none were born before."

John Calvin used the same counterargument in favor of Mary's perpetual virginity. In fact, in his *Harmony of the Gospels*, commenting on Matthew 1:25, he thought the contention of further siblings based on this passage was so unfounded that he wrote, "No man will obstinately keep up the argument, except from an extreme fondness for disputation."

In "Hebraic" use, the Greek *adelphos* applies to cousins, fellow countrymen, and a wide array of uses beyond the meaning of "sibling." Yet it is always translated as "brother" in the KJV (246 times). The cognate *adelphe* is translated twenty-four times only as "sister." This is because it reflects Hebrew usage, translated into Greek. Briefly put, in Jesus' Hebrew culture (and Middle Eastern culture even today), cousins were called "brothers."

Now, it's true that *sungenis* (Greek for "cousin") and its cognate *sungenia* appear in the New Testament fifteen times (*sungenia*: Luke 1:61; Acts 7:3, 14; *sungenis*: Mark 6:4; Luke 1:36, 58; 2:44; 14:12; 21:16; John 18:26; Acts 10:24; Rom. 9:3; 16:7, 11, 21). But in the KJV they are usually translated "kinsmen," "kinsfolk," or "kindred"—that is, in a sense wider than "cousin," often referring to the entire nation of Hebrews. Thus, the eminent Protestant linguist W. E. Vine, in his *Expository Dictionary of New Testament Words*, lists *sungenis* not only under "Cousin" but also under "Kin, Kinsfolk, Kinsman, Kinswoman."

In all but two of these occurrences, the authors were either Luke or Paul. Luke was a Greek Gentile. Paul, although Jewish, was raised in the very cosmopolitan, culturally Greek town of Tarsus. But even so, both still clearly used *adelphos* many times with the meaning of nonsibling (Luke 10:29, Acts 3:17; 7:23-26; Rom. 1:7, 13; 9:3; 1 Thess. 1:4).

Strikingly, it looks as if *every* time St. Paul uses *adelphos* (unless I missed one or two), he means it as something other than blood brother or sibling. He uses the word or related cognates no fewer than 138 times in this way. Yet we often hear about

Galatians 1:19: "James the Lord's brother." Despite the 137 other times that Paul uses *adelphos* to mean nonsibling, are we to believe that in this one case he *must* mean sibling? That doesn't make any sense.

Some folks think it is a compelling argument that *sungenis* isn't used to describe the brothers of Jesus. But they need to examine Mark 6:4, where *sungenis* appears:

> And Jesus said to them, "A prophet is not without honor, except in his own country, and among his own *kin*, and in his own house." (cf. John 7:5: "For even his brothers did not believe in him.")

What is the context? Let's look at the preceding verse, where the people in "his own country" (John 6:1) exclaimed:

> "Is not this the carpenter, the son of Mary and brother of James and Joses and Judas and Simon, and are not his sisters here with us?" And they took offense at him.

It can plausibly be argued, then, that Jesus' reference to *kin* (*sungenis*) refers (at least in part) back to this mention of His "brothers" and "sisters": His relatives. Since we know that *sungenis* refers to cousins or more distant relatives, that would be an indication of the status of those called Jesus' "brothers."

Jude is called the Lord's "brother" in Matthew 13:55 and Mark 6:3. If this is the same Jude who wrote the epistle bearing that name (as many think), he calls himself "a servant of Jesus Christ and brother of James" (Jude 1:1). Now, suppose for a moment that he *was* Jesus' blood brother. In that case, why would he refrain from referring to himself as the Lord's own sibling (while we are told that such a phraseology occurs several times in the New Testament, referring to a sibling relationship) and choose instead to identify himself as *James's* brother? Moreover, James also refrains from calling himself Jesus' brother, in his epistle (James 1:1: "servant of God and of the Lord Jesus Christ"), even though St. Paul calls him "the Lord's brother" (Gal. 1:19).

It's true that Scripture doesn't come right out and explicitly state that Mary was a perpetual virgin. But nothing in Scripture *contradicts* that notion, and (to say the same thing another way) nothing in the perpetual-virginity doctrine contradicts Scripture. Moreover, no Scripture can be produced that absolutely, undeniably, compellingly defeats the perpetual virginity of Mary.

The alleged disproofs utterly fail in their purpose. The attempted linguistic argument against Mary's perpetual virginity from the mere use of the word *brothers* in English translations (and from *sungenis*) falls flat at every turn, as we have seen.

If there is any purely "human" tradition here, then, it is the *denial* of the perpetual virginity of Mary, since it originated (mostly) some seventeen hundred years after the initial apostolic deposit—just as all heresies are much later corruptions. The earliest Church Fathers know of no such thing. To a person, they all testify that Mary was perpetually a virgin and, indeed, thought that this protected the doctrine of the Incarnation, as a miraculous birth from a mother who was a virgin before, during, and *after* the birth.

40

Mary's Consecrated Virginity

A priest who was helping a Baptist woman to understand the perpetual virginity of Mary became a bit frustrated, finally blurting out: "God Himself was in Mary's womb!" In a moment of illumination or grace or inspiration, the woman understood, thinking: "Take off your shoes, for this is holy ground." The many relevant biblical analogies took hold.

We observe in Holy Scripture, for instance, Uzziah, who died when he touched the ark of the covenant, which was arguably the holiest object in the Old Testament, even though he was only trying to prevent it from falling (2 Sam. 6:2-7). Others died by merely looking inside the ark (1 Sam. 6:19; cf. Exod. 33:20). When God was present in a special way on Mount Sinai, at the time Moses received the Ten Commandments (Exod. 19-20), the people were warned not even to touch the mountain or its border, lest they die (Exod. 19:12-13). This included even animals.

I submit that this has implications for the propriety (although not literal necessity) of Mary's being immaculate, in order to carry God in her womb for nine months. Without going into unnecessary detail, it also follows analogically, and from pious reflection, I think, that Mary's perpetual virginity is fitting

Mary's Consecrated Virginity

and proper by the nature of the relationship of a holy God and man.

The Blessed Virgin Mary became, in effect, the New Holy of Holies, where God specially resides. But in the case of Mary, God is more present than He ever was in the tabernacle and the Temple, because now He is there *physically*, as a man, as well. Mary is the ark of the new covenant (as the Church Fathers called her) and the Mother of God (the Son).

Similarly, Jesus taught us that there is no marriage in heaven (Matt. 22:30; Mark 12:25; Luke 20:34-35). Marriage is a type of the relationship of God and man and our eventual union (Eph. 5:21-33). The closeness that we will have with each other and with God in heaven is far more profound than mere physical proximity.

The denial of Mary's perpetual virginity (which was a radical innovation of the last 200 to 250 years, and *not* the view of the Protestant founders) exhibits an inadequate understanding of holy places. Consecrated persons and places are "set aside" for God's holy purposes.

Mary was perpetually a virgin not because normative married life is "bad" (a common unjust accusation against it) but rather, because consecrated virginity is a *higher* calling, and being the Mother of God is higher still.

Someone stated in a Facebook discussion that Catholic beliefs about Mary would mean she wasn't a "normal wife." I replied that Mary was anything *but* a "normal" Jewish wife in the first place. She was suddenly "with child" miraculously by the Holy Spirit and gave birth to Jesus: God the Son.

Most Protestants still accept the virgin birth. Consecrated virginity is far less notable than those two events. Yet the Incarnation and the virgin birth are widely accepted, while perpetual virginity is widely rejected. The traditional unity of the three related things is no longer comprehended by many.

Too many people assume that consecrated virginity is unimaginable or impossible, and that one could not possibly desire it. I think this prior assumption lies at the root of much of the objection. St. Paul (1 Cor. 7) maintains that the single state allows a higher, undistracted devotion to the Lord.

Why should we think, then, that the Mother of God would be any other than a perpetual virgin, devoted to God the Father, and her Son, God the Son?

The Blessed Virgin Mary was consecrated by God, with her consent. Some people are called to be "married to the Lord." It's precisely because we are so tied to the earth that we so often can't grasp heavenly realities that are clearly stated in Scripture (by both Jesus and Paul, in talking about singleness and voluntary eunuchs).

Some things can be so entirely appropriate that they almost approach necessity: not strictly logically but perhaps spiritually. Even the Crucifixion (and perhaps the Incarnation itself) was not *strictly* necessary (God *could* have simply declared those people saved who would have been saved by Jesus' death on the Cross), but they are sublimely important in the overall scheme of things.

God chose to save mankind by means of them. The virgin birth and Mary's perpetual virginity were the means that God chose to create the appropriate context in which the Incarnation occurred.

In Catholic thinking, and the ancient apostolic tradition, Mary's perpetual virginity is a protection, so to speak, of the miraculous nature of the Incarnation and Jesus' birth. It's a Christocentric doctrine: just as all Marian doctrines are.

Mary's Consecrated Virginity

But so many critics are almost obsessed with unfairly blasting the Catholic Church for supposedly raising Mary to an idolatrous state that they miss the fundamental reason for Marian beliefs: to exalt and focus on our Lord Jesus Christ.

41

A Rationalist Objection to the Virgin Birth

In Partu virginity refers to the belief that Jesus was born miraculously, without the usual physical travail of childbirth. Mary's virginity was preserved in the biological sense: i.e., the hymen remained intact.

Virginity, as classically understood, is not simply the absence of sexual activity (how we use the term today). It also had a literal physiological component (intact hymen). That's why, in order for the Blessed Virgin Mary to be a "perpetual virgin" in this sense, Jesus' birth (like His conception) had to be supernatural rather than natural. Jesus' conception, Incarnation, and *in partu* birth were all miraculous, although His being in Mary's womb for nine months obviously was natural. This is what the Catholic Church has taught.

A Catholic described objections to this belief (in either agreement or perplexity over) and stated that it would render the placenta and umbilical cord irrelevant, making Mary's pregnancy "appear as a fiction or myth or merely a play or a joke" and indeed, "comical." He thought the traditional Catholic view (which he thought entailed no implantation of the embryo in Mary's uterus) was "rationally in-congruent and ridiculous."

The Virgin Birth

He concluded that he wouldn't be able to defend the Catholic dogma if someone asked him about it. The following was my (off-the-cuff) reply:

Why would you think you have to explain every objection to every miracle that is believed in Christianity? These factors are no more "ridiculous" than the virgin birth itself, if we are to rank levels of supposed "implausibility."

This is a dogma. We believe by faith first; we don't have to "solve every problem" before we believe. That's not Christian faith, given by God's grace, but man-centered rationalism.

There are always "difficulties" and "problems" in any large system of thought. That doesn't prevent people from believing in the tenets of those systems. This includes physical science, where there are a host of things that remain unexplained (e.g., what caused the Big Bang; whether light is a particle or a wave, how life began, the complete lack of evidence for life anywhere else, et cetera). People don't disbelieve in the Big Bang because we can't explain *everything* about it.

Likewise with Catholic dogma. If even science requires faith and axiomatic presuppositions, how much more must religion, which is not identical to philosophy or reason in the first place? God could, for example, have simply made the placenta and umbilical cord disappear when the time came to be born (it doesn't mean they were never there or that there were no natural components). No biggie for Him — the One who parted the Red Sea, created the universe, and performed a host of other miracles.

This is the same sort of inconsistent thinking and false premise that causes folks to reject the physical, substantial presence of our Lord Jesus in the Eucharist, and Doubting Thomas to disbelieve that Jesus had risen, or those who won't believe unless they have some sign-miracle on demand.

Proving the Catholic Faith Is Biblical

All of this requires faith, and faith comes through grace accepted in free will. One can come up with any number of possible theories dealing with the placenta, and so forth, but I refuse to accept the premise that holds that we must do that in order to believe the dogma, and solving this "problem" is of little interest to me, even as an apologist. It's pretty low on the list of priorities.

We'd all be in very rough shape if our personal "epistemology" required us to know every jot and tittle of everything before we could believe it. Most things we do or believe in life we don't fully understand at all. One would have to argue that *every* miracle is "ridiculous" in the sense that it is unable to be consistently sustained. God's eternity and self-existence is absurd, *creatio ex nihilo* is, transubstantiation, the Hypostatic Union, the Resurrection, and on and on.

So why should a different, "superstandard" be applied to Christianity and particularly to Catholic dogma?

42

Martin Luther and the Immaculate Purification of Mary

My job as an apologist often involves defending aspects of Catholic belief that are "distinctive" over against Protestantism. We're asked why we believe thus-and-so, and the apologist steps in to provide some rationales and answers. But we also sometimes attempt to demonstrate *common ground*, and in so doing, in effect, assert, "See? We're not that different from you in *this* respect." This is a good thing, because it fosters Christian unity.

Thus, I will often cite some "Catholic" or nearly Catholic belief held by Martin Luther (1483-1546), the founder of Protestantism, in order to show that some doctrines are not *solely* Catholic, since the very originator of the system held it. In fact, I've studied Luther so closely that in some specific areas, I'd venture to say that not one in a thousand Lutherans would be familiar with what I've found.

One of the most fascinating of Luther's beliefs has to do with the question of Mary's Immaculate Conception (her being preserved from Original Sin from the moment of her conception). Luther had a rather "high" Mariology in many respects.

In 1522, he wrote in his *Little Prayer Book*: "She is full of grace [*voll Gnaden*]; so that she may be recognized as without any sin.... God's grace fills her with all gifts and frees her from all evil." In a 1527 sermon, preached "on the day of the Conception of Mary the Mother of God," Luther remarkably proclaimed:

> It is a sweet and pious belief that the infusion of Mary's soul was effected without original sin; so that in the very infusion of her soul she was also purified from original sin and adorned with God's gifts, receiving a pure soul infused by God; thus from the first moment she began to live she was free from all sin.[12]

As so often with Luther, however, his views evolve, or sometimes vacillate or contradict each other. This was the case on this point, though he remained *far* closer to the Catholic position than the general Protestant one.

In his *Disputation on the Divinity and Humanity of Christ*[13] (February 28, 1540), he placed Mary's "purification" at the *conception of Christ*: "In his conception all of Mary's flesh and blood was purified so that nothing sinful remained."

In 1543, in his work, *Vom Schem Hamphoras und vom Geschlecht Christi*, he affirmed that the Blessed Virgin Mary was "saved and purified from original sin through the Holy Spirit."[14] But he stated this without reference to *when* it occurred. We may plausibly infer that he continued to believe that it was at Christ's conception (given his 1540 statement).

The most fascinating aspect of all this, in my opinion, is that St. Thomas Aquinas had expressed something very similar, almost three centuries earlier:

---

[12] Catholic biographer Hartmann Grisar's translation, 1917.
[13] February 28, 1540; 1992 translation by Lutheran Eric W. Gritsch.
[14] 2004 translation by historian Beth Kreitzer.

Martin Luther and the Immaculate Purification

The second purification effected in her by the Holy Ghost was by means of the conception of Christ which was the operation of the Holy Ghost. And in respect of this, it may be said that He purified her entirely from the fomes [i.e., the stain of sin].[15]

Luther was actually following a strain of Catholic scholastic thought that the Church at length deemed as erroneous. Yes, even St. Thomas Aquinas could occasionally be mistaken!

Can it be said, then, in summary, that Luther was "opposed" to the Catholic dogma of the Immaculate Conception: fully defined at the highest level of dogmatic certainty, in 1854, by Blessed Pope Pius IX?

Well, yes and no. If we mean the dogma as it is believed by the Catholic Church, and the *timing* of God's special act of grace (at Mary's own conception), he eventually *denied that aspect* of it, but if we mean "removal of Original Sin," which is the essence and heart of the doctrine, then he did *not* deny it.

Luther *never* believed that the act occurred at Mary's *conception*, because he originally thought it occurred at *ensoulment*, which he separated from conception (as most people — including St. Thomas Aquinas — still did in the late Middle Ages). The timing in his view simply shifted from the time of ensoulment to the time of (or shortly before) Christ's conception.

The common ground in his views is God's removal of Original Sin from Mary by a special act of grace, and he seems to think that she was free of all actual sin, too, after Christ's conception. These two things, as far as they go, are very "Catholic" indeed!

---

[15] St. Thomas Aquinas, *Summa Theologica*, III, Q. 27, art. 3.

Proving the Catholic Faith Is Biblical

In light of a consideration of all the relevant evidence, I think it's accurate to refer to Luther's fully developed position as Mary's *Immaculate Purification*. It's not identical to the Catholic position (which wasn't yet a Catholic dogma during his lifetime), but it is far more similar to it than to any denominational Protestant position today, including that of Lutheranism.

43

Mary's Immaculate Conception

Are there explicit, "direct" *proofs* of the Immaculate Conception of the Blessed Virgin Mary in the Bible? No. Does the Bible ever teach that all doctrines must be *explicitly* contained in it? No. Is this doctrine *harmonious* with what is in Scripture and supported by analogy and plausibility? Yes.

> **Luke 1:28**: And he came to her and said, "Hail, O favored one, the Lord is with you!" [In the RSV, Catholic edition, "favored one" is rendered as "full of grace."]

Many translations use "favor" here, yet even the great Baptist Greek scholar A. T. Robertson[16] agrees that the word involved (*kecharitomene*) means "full of grace which thou hast received." It's derived from the Greek root *charis* (grace). Presbyterian Greek scholar Marvin R. Vincent agrees that it means "endued with grace."[17]

Now, a Catholic asks, "What does it mean to be *full* of grace?" For St. Paul, grace is the antithesis and overcomer of sin:

---

[16] A. T. Robertson, *Word Pictures in the New Testament* (Nashville: Broadman Press, 1930), vol. 2, 13.
[17] *Word Studies in the New Testament*, vol. 1, 259.

Proving the Catholic Faith Is Biblical

Romans 6:14, 19, 22: For sin will have no dominion over you, since you are not under law but under grace ... so now yield your members to righteousness for sanctification.... But now that you have been set free from sin ... the return you get is sanctification and its end, eternal life.

Moreover, we are *saved* by grace:

Ephesians 2:8: For by grace you have been saved through faith; and this is not your own doing, it is the gift of God. (cf. Acts 15:11; Rom. 3:24; Titus 2:11; 3:7)

It follows, I submit, that for a person to be *full* of grace is to both be saved and to be exceptionally, completely holy. Therefore, Mary is holy and sinless. The essence of the Immaculate Conception is sinlessness, and this is deduced from many biblical passages about the antithetical relation of grace to sin, and salvation and its accompanying sanctification to sin.

The only remaining question is: *When* did God apply this grace to Mary? We know she possessed it as a young woman, at the Annunciation. Catholics believe that God gave her the grace at her conception so as to avoid the Original Sin that she inevitably would have inherited, being human, *but* for God's preventive grace, which saved her from falling into the pit of sin.

But do we ever observe in the Bible, persons being extraordinarily sanctified, even before their birth, as we believe Mary was? Yes, we do; for example, the prophets Isaiah and Jeremiah:

Isaiah 49:1, 5: The LORD called me from the womb.... And now the LORD says, who formed me from the womb to be his servant, to bring Jacob back to him, and that

Mary's Immaculate Conception

Israel might be gathered to him, for I am honored in the eyes of the LORD. (cf. Job 31:15, 18; Judges 16:17)

Jeremiah 1:5: Before I formed you in the womb I knew you, and before you were born I consecrated you; I appointed you a prophet to the nations. (cf. Sir. 49:7)

"Consecrated" or "sanctified" (KJV) in Jeremiah 1:5 is the Hebrew word *quadash* (Strong's word no. 6942). According to Gesenius's *Hebrew-Chaldee Lexicon of the Old Testament* (p. 725), in this instance it meant "to declare any one holy." Jeremiah was thus consecrated or sanctified from the womb; possibly from conception. This is fairly analogous to the doctrine of the Immaculate Conception. We know Jeremiah was a very holy man. Was he sinless, though? Perhaps he was. We also have New Testament evidence of such sanctification before birth (John the Baptist and St. Paul):

Luke 1:15: [F]or he will be great before the Lord, and he shall drink no wine nor strong drink, and he will be filled with the Holy Spirit, even from his mother's womb. (cf. Luke 1:41, 44)

Galatians 1:15: he who had set me apart before I was born, and had called me through his grace.

We know that John the Baptist was also a very holy man. Was he sinless? We can't know that *for sure* from the biblical data. St. Catherine of Siena, for one, believed that he never sinned (*A Treatise of Prayer*). But we do know for sure that he was sanctified from the womb.

Therefore, by analogy and plausibility, we can and may conclude that it is "biblical" to believe in faith that Mary was

Proving the Catholic Faith Is Biblical

immaculately conceived. Nothing in the Bible *contradicts* this belief. It does require *faith*, of course. God restored to Mary the innocence that Eve had before the Fall and filled her with grace in order to prepare her for her unspeakably sublime, sanctified task as the Mother of God the Son. Why should He *not* do so?

44

Mary Is the Mother of God

1. Jesus called Himself the "Son of God":

   John 10:36: "[D]o you say of him whom the Father consecrated and sent into the world, 'You are blaspheming,' because I said, 'I am the Son of God'?"

2. "Son of God" means the same as "God" in the Jewish mind:

   John 5:18: This was why the Jews sought all the more to kill him, because he not only broke the sabbath but also called God his Father, making himself equal with God.

3. The Blessed Virgin Mary is the Mother of the Son of God; therefore (see number 2), she is the Mother of God:

   Luke 1:31-32, 35: And behold, you will conceive in your womb and bear a son, and you shall call his name Jesus. He will be great, and will be called the Son of the Most High.... And the angel said to her, "The Holy Spirit will come upon you, and the power of the Most High will overshadow you; therefore the child to be born will be called holy, the Son of God."

Here is also a second way to establish Mary as the Mother of God (*Theotokos* in Greek):

Luke 1:43: And why is this granted me, that the mother of my Lord [*kurios*] should come to me?

John 20:28: Thomas answered him, "My Lord [*kurios*] and my God [*theos*]!"

"Lord [*kurios*] God [*theos*]": Luke 1:6, 32, 68; 4:8, 12; 10:27; 20:37. Therefore, "Lord [*kurios*] equals God [*theos*]. Jesus is called both in John 20:28. Mary is the Mother of the Lord (Luke 1:43). Therefore, she is the mother of God, since *Lord* = *God*. Case closed.

We don't say of mothers that they are the mother of their child's *body*, but of the child, and the child has a body and a soul. The mothers didn't create the soul; God did. Likewise, with Jesus: Mary is the Mother of Jesus, who is God the Son. Thus, she is the Mother of God. It's wrong and even illogical to say she was the mother of His body. No; she was the mother of the Divine Person, Jesus, who had a human nature and also a divine nature (that she had nothing to do with).

But she is still the mother of the Person, regardless of that, as any mother is the mother of a person who has a soul directly created by God.

45

The Assumption of the Blessed Virgin Mary

Our Protestant friends in Christ often challenge us to find "proofs" of our doctrines in the Bible. When it comes to the doctrine of the Assumption, almost all of them think or say, "There is *nothing whatever* in the Bible about *that*!"

I'd like to examine this question from two perspectives: whether the challenge they make is itself based on a biblical model, and whether we can find anything in Scripture to support our dogmatic belief in Mary's bodily Assumption into heaven.

The assumption (no pun intended!) casually made by those who argue in this way is the notion that all doctrines believed by Christians must be *explicitly* mentioned in Scripture. This is a key aspect of the Protestant foundational belief in *sola Scriptura* (Scripture is the *only infallible* authority or rule of faith).

But the Bible, in fact, *never teaches* this idea (nor *sola Scriptura* itself). Protestants can't prove it from Scripture. Moreover, there are other doctrines held by Protestants, too, based on no biblical indications at all. One clear example is the canon of Scripture. The Bible never lists its own books. The Bible's table of contents comes entirely from Christian Tradition.

Yet Protestants accept it (minus seven books); and this is contrary to *sola Scriptura*. Despite all this, we are unreasonably

Proving the Catholic Faith Is Biblical

asked to prove everything we believe as Catholics, from explicit biblical passages.

Catholics believe that all Catholic and Christian doctrines must be in harmony with Scripture, that they must not contradict it, and that some doctrines are able to be supported only indirectly, implicitly, or by deduction from other related Bible passages.

All Catholic doctrines have scriptural support in *some* sense (this is my main specialty as an apologist). We also believe in sacred tradition: itself always in harmony with Scripture. Sometimes (as in the present case), a doctrine is "stronger" in tradition.

I agree that there is no *direct* proof of Mary's Assumption in Scripture. But there is strong deductive and analogical evidence. The deductive argument has to do with the consequences of Mary's Immaculate Conception: a doctrine more directly indicated in Scripture (e.g., Luke 1:28).

Bodily death and decay are the result of sin and the Fall of man (Gen. 3:16-19; Ps. 16:10). An absence of actual and Original Sin would allow for instant bodily resurrection. It's as if Mary goes back to before the Fall (for this reason the Church Fathers call her the New Eve).

Jesus' Resurrection makes possible universal resurrection (1 Cor. 15:13, 16) and the redemption of our bodies as well as souls (1 Cor. 15:20-23). Mary's Assumption is the "firstfruits," sign, and type of the general resurrection of all (created) mankind; she exemplifies the age in which death and sin are conquered once and for all (1 Cor. 15:26).

The analogical argument is a second line of approach: biblical examples that have strong similarity in important respects to Mary's bodily Assumption. Here are five such analogies:

The Assumption of the Blessed Virgin Mary

2 Kings 2:1, 11: [T]he LORD was about to *take Elijah up* to heaven by a whirlwind.... And Elijah *went up* by a whirlwind *into heaven.*

2 Corinthians 12:2-3: I know a man in Christ [i.e., Paul himself] who fourteen years ago was *caught up to the third heaven.*... And I know that this man was *caught up into Paradise* — whether *in the body* or out of the body I do not know, God knows.

1 Thessalonians 4:16-17: And the dead in Christ will *rise* first; then we who are alive, who are left, shall be *caught up together with them in the clouds* to meet the Lord in the air; and so we shall always be with the Lord.

Hebrews 11:5: By faith Enoch was *taken up* so that he should not see death, and he was not found, because God had *taken* him. (cf. Gen. 5:24)

Revelation 11:11-12: But after the three and a half days a breath of life from God entered them, and they stood up on their feet.... Then they heard a loud voice from heaven saying to them, "*Come up* hither!" And in the sight of their foes *they went up to heaven in a cloud.*

In three of these instances, the person didn't die (in one, the person even came back); in two, the persons died first. The Church hasn't declared whether Mary died. All these events occur by virtue of the *power of God*, not the *intrinsic ability* of the persons.

Jesus ascended by His own power, but the Blessed Virgin Mary was assumed by the power of her Son Jesus' victory over death. Hers was an immediate resurrection. One day all who are saved will be bodily resurrected. Mary was the first after the Resurrection — quite appropriately (and even, I submit, expected), since she was Jesus' own Mother.

46

Mary the Queen Mother and Queen of Heaven

The standard Catholic apologetics argument in defense of Mary as the queen mother and Queen of Heaven is based on the analogy of the practice of the ancient kings of Judah, who made their mothers, rather than their wives, queens. Thus, Solomon, the son of David, had his mother (Bathsheba) as queen, and she even had a throne next to his, at his right hand (1 Kings 2:19). And as the queen mother, she could make requests of him. The queen mother also wore a crown (Jer. 13:18).

By analogy, we argue that Mary, as the Mother of God and Queen of Heaven, can be sought in intercession, in order to ask her Son a request; and that her requests have great power because of her exalted position in the kingdom (James 5:16).

It's an analogy, but (as many are) an imperfect one, because Bathsheba (being a sinner like the rest of us, and once an adulteress) would not always ask for the right thing, whereas Mary (being sinless and perfected in heaven and rather unique and exalted among creatures) *would*. The analogy is to the *office*, not every single jot and tittle.

It's like arguing for the office of the papacy by the original example of Peter and the prototype that he provided in the

Proving the Catholic Faith Is Biblical

Bible. The office of the papacy is not in the slightest undermined because Peter betrayed Jesus, or because he was once rebuked by Jesus, who said, "Get behind me, Satan" (Matt. 16:23) or because Paul rebuked him for hypocrisy. Nor does this undermine papal infallibility, which is a limited charism, and not directly connected with whether the particular pope involved is a sinner.

Likewise, biblical inspiration is not undermined because God used sinners to write His inspired Bible (murderers such as Moses, David, and Paul, and betrayers and wimps such as Peter; former despised tax collectors such as Matthew). The "office" of Scripture writer, in other words, was not rendered null and void because sinners occupied it.

Another similar imperfect analogy would be King David (the adulterer and murderer) as a type, shadow, or forerunner of the Messiah, Jesus. This is a clear scriptural motif in the prophets (Isa. 9:6-7; Jer. 23:5-6; 30:9; Ezek. 34:23-24; 37:24-25; Zech. 12:8; cf. Luke 1:31-33, 68-69). His sin did not render the covenant God made with him null and void (provided that he sincerely repented: as he in fact did). He (a great sinner) remained the prototype for the Messiah.

By the same token, Bathsheba could be a prototype for and analogy of Mary as queen mother, even though a sinner herself (as we all are).

47

The Virgin Mary in the Book of Revelation

Revelation 12:1-6, 13, 17: And a great portent appeared in heaven, a woman clothed with the sun, with the moon under her feet, and on her head a crown of twelve stars; she was with child and she cried out in her pangs of birth, in anguish for delivery. And another portent appeared in heaven; behold, a great red dragon, with seven heads and ten horns, and seven diadems upon his heads. His tail swept down a third of the stars of heaven, and cast them to the earth. And the dragon stood before the woman who was about to bear a child, that he might devour her child when she brought it forth; she brought forth a male child, one who is to rule all the nations with a rod of iron, but her child was caught up to God and to his throne, and the woman fled into the wilderness, where she has a place prepared by God, in which to be nourished for one thousand two hundred and sixty days.... And when the dragon saw that he had been thrown down to the earth, he pursued the woman who had borne the male child.... Then the dragon was angry with the woman, and went off to make war on the rest of her offspring, on those who keep the

Proving the Catholic Faith Is Biblical

commandments of God and bear testimony to Jesus. And he stood on the sand of the sea.

The woman's son is described as "one who is to rule all the nations with a rod of iron, but her child was caught up to God and to his throne" (Rev. 12:5). Can it be plausibly denied that this is Jesus? If it isn't Jesus, who is it? And if it is, then how can anyone deny that His mother is Mary? Catholics believe that there is a double application here to the Church and to Mary (a common phenomenon in Scripture). But to deny the application to Mary altogether runs into the exegetical absurdities. Here are relevant cross-references:

Psalm 2:7-9: I will tell of the decree of the LORD: He said to me, "You are my son, today I have begotten you. Ask of me, and I will make the nations your heritage, and the ends of the earth your possession. You shall *break them with a rod of iron*, and dash them in pieces like a potter's vessel."

Revelation 19:13-15: He is clad in a robe dipped in blood, and the name by which he is called is The Word of God. And the armies of heaven, arrayed in fine linen, white and pure, followed him on white horses. From his mouth issues a sharp sword with which to smite the nations, and he will *rule them with a rod of iron*; he will tread the wine press of the fury of the wrath of God the Almighty.

Protestant commentators agree as well. Baptist A. T. Robertson says of Rev. 12:5: "There is here, of course, direct reference to the birth of Jesus from Mary." *Eerdmans Bible Commentary* likewise states: "The 'catching up' is sufficiently similar to the victorious ascension of Jesus to make plain its real meaning in this context."

The Virgin Mary in the Book of Revelation

Jamieson, Fausset, and Brown Commentary states: "rod of iron ... ch. 2:27; Psalm 2:9, which passages prove the Lord Jesus to be meant. Any interpretation which ignores this must be wrong." It also notes the reference to the Ascension.

It can have a double application to the Church as well, but if we're talking about Jesus' Mother, that has to be Mary, because Jesus wasn't *born of* the Church; He *set up* the Church.

48

Biblical Analogies for Marian Apparitions

By analogy, biblical accounts of "appearances" of those who have died are of the same essential nature as a Marian apparition. Angels (i.e., creatures, like men) might also be included in such a survey, but stories of angels are relatively well known, and for the sake of closer analogy and brevity, I have selected only passages with men or the appearance of men. Several of these passages involve foretelling of the future, in a manner not unlike that of the apparitions at Fátima in 1917. And several historical figures are named as appearing after death (Samuel, Onias, Jeremiah, Moses, and Elijah).

1 Samuel 28:12-15: When *the woman saw Samuel*, she cried out with a loud voice; and the woman said to Saul, "Why have you deceived me? You are Saul." The king said to her, "Have no fear; what do you see?" And the woman said to Saul, "I see a god coming up out of the earth." He said to her, "What is his appearance?" And she said, "An old man is coming up; and he is wrapped in a robe." *And Saul knew that it was Samuel,* and he bowed with his face to the ground, and did obeisance. *Then Samuel said*

Biblical Analogies for Marian Apparitions

to Saul, "Why have you disturbed me by bringing me up?" Saul answered, "I am in great distress; for the Philistines are warring against me, and God has turned away from me and answers me no more, either by prophets or by dreams; therefore I have summoned you to tell me what I shall do."

Ezekiel 40:3-4: When he brought me there, behold, there was *a man, whose appearance was like bronze*, with a line of flax and a measuring reed in his hand; and he was standing in the gateway. And the man said to me, "Son of man, look with your eyes, and hear with your ears, and set your mind upon all that I shall show you, for you were brought here in order that I might show it to you; declare all that you see to the house of Israel."

Daniel 8:15-19: When I, Daniel, had seen the vision, I sought to understand it; and behold, *there stood before me one having the appearance of a man*. And I heard a man's voice between the banks of the Ulai, and it called, "Gabriel, make this man understand the vision." So he came near where I stood; and when he came, I was frightened and fell upon my face. But he said to me, "Understand, O son of man, that the vision is for the time of the end." As he was speaking to me, I fell into a deep sleep with my face to the ground; but he touched me and set me on my feet. He said, "Behold, I will make known to you what shall be at the latter end of the indignation; for it pertains to the appointed time of the end."

Daniel 10:4-21: On the twenty-fourth day of the first month, as I was standing on the bank of the great river, that is, the Tigris, I lifted up my eyes and looked, and behold, *a man clothed in linen*, whose loins were girded with gold of Uphaz. His body was like beryl, *his face like the appearance of lightning, his eyes like flaming torches*, his arms and legs like the gleam of burnished bronze, and the sound of his words like the noise of a multitude. And I, Daniel, alone saw the vision, for the men who were with me did not see the vision, but a great trembling fell upon them, and they fled to hide themselves. So I was left alone and saw this great vision, and no strength was left in me; my radiant appearance was fearfully changed, and I retained no strength. Then I heard the sound of his words; and when I heard the sound of his words, I fell on my face in a deep sleep with my face to the ground. And behold, a hand touched me and set me trembling on my hands and knees. And he said to me, "O Daniel, man greatly beloved, give heed to the words that I speak to you, and stand upright, for now *I have been sent to you*." While he was speaking this word to me, I stood up trembling. Then he said to me, "Fear not, Daniel, for from the first day that you set your mind to understand and humbled yourself before your God, your words have been heard, and I have come because of your words. The prince of the kingdom of Persia withstood me twenty-one days; but Michael, one of the chief princes, came to help me, so I left him there with the prince of the kingdom of Persia and *came to make you understand what is to befall your people in the latter days. For the vision is for days yet to come*." When he had spoken to me according to these words, I turned my face toward the ground and was dumb. And behold, one in the likeness of the sons

Biblical Analogies for Marian Apparitions

of men touched my lips; then I opened my mouth and spoke. I said to him who stood before me, "O my lord, by reason of the vision pains have come upon me, and I retain no strength. How can my lord's servant talk with my lord? For now no strength remains in me, and no breath is left in me." Again one having the appearance of a man touched me and strengthened me. And he said, "O man greatly beloved, fear not, peace be with you; be strong and of good courage." And when he spoke to me, I was strengthened and said, "Let my lord speak, for you have strengthened me." Then he said, *"Do you know why I have come to you?* But now I will return to fight against the prince of Persia; and when I am through with him, lo, the prince of Greece will come. But I will tell you what is inscribed in the book of truth: there is none who contends by my side against these except Michael, your prince."

Sirach 46:19-20: Before the time of his eternal sleep, *Samuel* called men to witness before the Lord and his anointed: "I have not taken any one's property, not so much as a pair of shoes." And no man accused him. *Even after he had fallen asleep he prophesied and revealed to the king his death, and lifted up his voice out of the earth in prophecy,* to blot out the wickedness of the people.

2 Maccabees 5:1-4: About this time Antiochus made his second invasion of Egypt. And it happened that over all the city, for almost forty days, *there appeared golden-clad horsemen charging through the air,* in companies fully armed with lances and drawn swords — troops of horsemen drawn up, attacks and counterattacks made on this side

Proving the Catholic Faith Is Biblical

and on that, brandishing of shields, massing of spears, hurling of missiles, the flash of golden trappings, and armor of all sorts. Therefore all men prayed that the apparition might prove to have been a good omen.

2 Maccabees 10:29-30: When the battle became fierce, *there appeared to the enemy from heaven five resplendent men on horses with golden bridles*, and they were leading the Jews. Surrounding Maccabeus and protecting him with their own armor and weapons, they kept him from being wounded. And they showered arrows and thunderbolts upon the enemy, so that, confused and blinded, they were thrown into disorder and cut to pieces.

2 Maccabees 15:11-16: He armed each of them not so much with confidence in shields and spears as with the inspiration of brave words, and he cheered them all by relating *a dream, a sort of vision*, which was worthy of belief. *What he saw was this: Onias, who had been high priest*, a noble and good man, of modest bearing and gentle manner, one who spoke fittingly and had been trained from childhood in all that belongs to excellence, was praying with outstretched hands for the whole body of the Jews. Then likewise a man appeared, distinguished by his gray hair and dignity, and of marvelous majesty and authority. And *Onias spoke, saying, "This is a man who loves the brethren and prays much for the people and the holy city, Jeremiah, the prophet of God."* Jeremiah stretched out his right hand and gave to Judas a golden sword, and as he gave it he addressed him thus: *"Take this holy sword, a gift from God, with which you will strike down your adversaries."*

Biblical Analogies for Marian Apparitions

Matthew 17:1-4: And after six days Jesus took with him Peter and James and John his brother, and led them up a high mountain apart. And he was transfigured before them, and his face shone like the sun, and his garments became white as light. And behold, *there appeared to them Moses and Elijah, talking with him*. And Peter said to Jesus, "Lord, it is well that we are here; if you wish, I will make three booths here, one for you and one for *Moses* and one for *Elijah*." (cf. Mark 9:4-5)

Matthew 27:51-53: And behold, the curtain of the temple was torn in two, from top to bottom; and the earth shook, and the rocks were split; *the tombs also were opened, and many bodies of the saints who had fallen asleep were raised*, and coming out of the tombs after his resurrection *they went into the holy city and appeared to many*.

Acts 16:9: And *a vision appeared to Paul* in the night: *a man of Macedonia* was standing beseeching him and saying, "Come over to Macedonia and help us."

Revelation 4:4: Round the throne were twenty-four thrones, and seated on the thrones were *twenty-four elders, clad in white garments*, with golden crowns upon their heads. (cf. Rev. 4:10; 5:5-14; 7:11, 13; 11:16; 14:3; 19:4)

Revelation 6:9-10: When he opened the fifth seal, *I saw under the altar the souls of those who had been slain for the word of God* and for the witness they had borne; they cried out with a loud voice, "O Sovereign Lord, holy and true, how long before thou wilt judge and avenge our blood on those who dwell upon the earth?" (cf. Rev. 11:3-13)

49

Protestant Difficulties Regarding Papal Infallibility

Popes can err if they are not talking in the limited circumstances in which we believe papal infallibility applies to them, per the 1870 dogma. The pope is not some kind of inspired oracle, like a walking Bible. If, for example, the pope said over lunch, "The earth is flat," that would not be in line with the special conditions of what we define as "infallible" because it was merely a private remark and has nothing to do with faith or morals.

If the pope wrote an encyclical, however, and stated, "I define and declare *ex cathedra*, as pope, speaking for all Catholics, that henceforth, all the Catholic faithful must regard the earth as flat," then this would be a crisis for Catholics, since it would be a blatant example of a falsehood promulgated under the proper conditions, thus overthrowing the dogma.

We say that this has never happened. If we look at the very "best" case our critics come up with, Pope Honorius, we find that he was making a statement in a private letter.[18] Right off

---

[18] Pope Honorius, who reigned from 625-638, used imprecise language regarding the heresy of Monothelitism, which held that Christ had one will, combining the divine and human wills. He

Protestant Difficulties Regarding Infallibility

the bat, then, it had nothing to do with infallibility. Their best case is literally a non sequitur: it doesn't disprove infallibility in the slightest.

Proper definitions are crucial in any debate. On this issue, that seems to be about 75 percent of the battle. Folks don't want to accept Catholic explanations and want almost to rewrite the dogma according to their own whims. I understand that. I played that game myself in 1990 when I detested infallibility and thought it was the most ridiculous thing in the world (or at least in theology). But that game is ultimately an intellectually dishonest endeavor.

Protestants seem often unable to distinguish infallibility from inspiration. This is the main problem of comprehension, I suspect. It's understandable, because it's a new thing. The Protestant outlook is diametrically opposed to infallibility because it is so contrary to *sola Scriptura*: one of the two pillars of the so-called Reformation. That's why I fought it so ferociously myself: because I was a huge *sola Scriptura* guy and Luther devotee to boot, and I had already been doing apologetics for nine years, so I loved to argue and dispute.

---

did this merely in a personal letter to a patriarch, rather than a magisterial document, binding the entire Church. He was condemned by the Third Ecumenical Council of Constantinople (the sixth ecumenical council: 680-681). But Pope Leo II, in his affirmation of the council, made it clear, in explanation, that Honorius had neither *embraced* nor *endorsed* the heresy but, rather, was only negligent in not condemning it. In any event, since he did not declare a heresy as true and binding, his error had nothing whatsoever to do with papal infallibility (as Catholics define or understand it); therefore, this cannot be regarded in any way, shape, matter, or form, as a *disproof* of that Catholic dogma.

Proving the Catholic Faith Is Biblical

It comes back to prior premises. You can't look at infallibility from Protestant eyes. You have to try to understand it from Catholic eyes, even though not yet Catholic. We always see things through our own premises, so to change them provisionally, to grasp another, is difficult. It's like debate, too. To debate well, one should understand the opposing position at least as well as his opponent does. And that takes a lot of work and sort of a mental discipline.

It seems overdramatic (in *ex cathedra* statements such as those concerning the Immaculate Conception and Assumption of Mary), to say that whoever disbelieves has fallen away from the Faith, et cetera, but again, one has to understand that Catholics believe that we have to accept all that the Church teaches; therefore, if a pronouncement at this high level is made, it has to be accepted, lest we have destroyed the principle of Catholic authority, and in that sense have rejected the Catholic Faith.

The opposite of this is the "cafeteria Catholic" game that liberal dissidents play. This is like a Protestant rejecting *sola Scriptura*. One who did so wouldn't be much of a Protestant anymore.

To use the analogy of government, it's the difference between having an idea for a bill and having a bill drawn from that thought passing the House and Senate and being signed into law by the president. The second is binding as law; the first is not at all. The president or Senate Leader or House Speaker might have talked about a proposed bill, but it has no binding force when it is simply being talked about. When it is made a law, it does have binding power.

So what we're saying is that when the pope binds the entire faithful to a dogma and declares that it is to be held by all Catholics, we believe in faith in such cases that he is given by God the gift of infallibility: protection from error.

Protestant Difficulties Regarding Infallibility

If the objection is that it is fideism with no objective proof, then we appeal to history and show how alleged counterfactuals such as Honorius don't succeed and that no such scenarios have succeeded in disproving papal infallibility.

Most Protestants (especially if they're like I used to be) simply assume that such a thing is impossible. They lack faith in God's capacity to enact His supernatural gifts in men.

I reply that it takes much more faith to believe in the inspiration of Scripture (that the huge amount of words in the Bible are not self-contradictory and are all "God-breathed") than infallibility in limited circumstances, so that if one is believed, the other should not be all that difficult to accept in faith.

God had to use lousy sinners such as Moses and David and Paul and Peter and Matthew to write the Bible. What else did He have: except for a few recorded words from sinless Mary? Thus, sin and the foibles and follies of men are no barrier to Him if He has some purpose (He even used a donkey once). Protestants forget that these inspired words in Scripture were written by very human and sinful men, as we all are. They came from men, just as papal decrees come from men.

All those objections make no sense analogically. If one thing is believed, the other should not be impossible to accept. The real root of the error, I believe, is in the *sola Scriptura* mentality, which holds (with no biblical support) that only the Bible is infallible and that no human institutions (Church, popes, councils) can be, because only the Bible is, because the Bible says so (but in fact it never does, and it states the contrary). That is where the root error and circular reasoning lies.

50

Why It Is Easy to Know What Catholics Should Believe

I contend that Catholic teachings are abundantly clear, as to what the faithful Catholic is required to believe or disbelieve. All such teachings are plainly laid out, especially now in the *Catechism*. Virtually all the important theological issues have already been worked through and worked out by minds far greater than ours, by the guidance of the Holy Spirit. We don't have to work that hard to understand. We simply look it up and believe it, on the authority of the Church. The only things that are up in the air are matters of the utmost mystery, that humans can barely understand at all, such as the internal Catholic predestination debate. But that has no bearing on practical, day-to-day Catholic living anyway.

It's not necessary to interpret infallibly; it is necessary only to know and believe by faith, based on many cumulative, converging evidences, that there is an infallible authority. One simply accepts that. It's not a game of philosophy, but of religious faith, grounded in reason and the Bible and historical precedent.

The teachings are authoritative, if they come down to us from papal encyclicals, ecumenical councils, or the *Catechism*. All the fine-tuning and hair-splitting distinctions are for scholars

What Catholics Should Believe

and theologians and apologists to have fun arguing about; that's what they get paid to do. But that has little relevance for Joe Q. Catholic.

The Protestant "infallibility regress" argument in apologetics states that the individual Catholic still needs to interpret even an infallible decree. Therefore, he is in no better epistemological position than the Protestant, because he is not an infallible interpreter, and whether decrees are in fact infallible does not overcome the problem (so we're told).

But this approach fails, because *Christianity is not philosophy*. One cannot achieve airtight, mathematical certainty in matters of faith. The Catholic authority structure is quite sufficient for us, as it was for the apostles and Fathers.

It's always easy to take swipes at the Big Red Barn of Catholicism. But the question is: What is the better *alternative*? Then, when we see how Protestants try to resolve authority problems, it gets truly self-defeating and absurd. That's not true of Catholicism. It's not philosophically airtight, but very few things are. Still, our system of theology and ecclesiology doesn't break down and become logically self-defeating, as all forms of Protestantism do, the more they are scrutinized.

The Catholic is not advocating absolute philosophical certainty (a thing that is generally rare as it is), but rather, the certitude of faith, based on many converging evidences of many sorts.

I deny that it is difficult to determine what Catholics believe and *must* believe. Anyone who can read and exercise rudimentary logic can understand what the Church teaches, from the *Catechism*. It's easy for critics to talk in generalities and try to cast doubt on everything, just as agnostics do with Christianity and the Bible. But unless they get down to particulars and show

Proving the Catholic Faith Is Biblical

how the Catholic system fails in those examples and, moreover, demonstrate that they are important enough examples to be relevant to a debate about whether Catholicism or Protestantism has a more coherent and workable rule of faith and authority structure, they haven't accomplished anything.

One can play philosophical skeptic all day long; it's a fun game, but irrelevant to the discussion, since Christianity (in any form — not just Catholic) is not a mere philosophy or rationalistic exercise. It is a religious faith and requires a reasoned (not irrational) faith. Faith is not mathematical demonstration.

The premises of the "infallibility regress" argument are absurd to begin with, because it has to assume the untruth (Christianity is mere philosophy and operates totally on that plane where it comes to determination of true doctrine) even to make the argument. Whether the one who argues in this way is aware of it or not, that's what the premise amounts to. I deny the premise, and I think that anyone who would only examine it more closely would also deny it.

All anyone has to do to understand Catholicism is know how to read and have the faith and willingness to accept what the *Catechism* proclaims. I think a lack of faith is really the bottom line with Protestants who reject Catholic claims. They don't have enough faith to believe that God could and does protect a Church, which is a human institution, and Christian apostolic doctrine. They have the faith to believe in the higher, more involved gift of the *inspiration* of human sinners (Scripture) but not the lesser and far more limited gift of *infallibility* of human sinners (a pope and ecumenical councils and apostolic succession and sacred tradition). Even that makes no sense. They have great faith in one instance that requires *more* faith and have none (and outright skepticism) where *less* faith is required.

What Catholics Should Believe

We aren't making the individual the final arbiter of true doctrine, as Protestants do. To posit and believe by faith in an infallible Church makes perfect sense, because Christians already believe in an inspired Scripture, and that Scripture has much indication of an infallible Church. That is consistent.

But to fall back on a mere noninfallible individual believer, who supposedly will figure all this stuff out, or else have to operate in a sort of limbo or agnostic or uncertain state in their Christian life, is not only absurd and perfectly implausible in the abstract, but chaotic in actual practice, as history has amply shown.

The fact remains that there is no chaos with regard to Catholic doctrine, for those willing to accept what the Church has clearly proclaimed, whereas there is plenty within Protestantism. The "infallibility regress" game falls flat every time, when properly scrutinized. And it is very laborious and time-consuming. Disproving error is always a lot harder than assertion of error.

51

The Bible Never Says That Jesus Is God? Wrong!

We apologists hear every fable, myth, and tall tale regarding theology that anyone could ever imagine. I've heard this one for over thirty years. In fact, one of my first research projects in the early '80s, after I took up apologetics (back in my evangelical days), was to collect biblical passages that provide evidence for the Holy Trinity and the deity, or divinity, of Jesus Christ.

I'd like to highlight a few of the more obvious, undeniable, plain passages, to counter those who make such negative claims.

> **John 1:1, 14**: In the beginning was the Word, and the Word was with God, and the Word was God. ... And the Word became flesh and dwelt among us, full of grace and truth; we have beheld his glory, glory as of the only Son from the Father.

This is one of the most well-known "prooftexts." Jesus is eternal (here, "beginning" means "eternity past"). He was with God the Father and is God the Son. To make sure that the reader has no misunderstanding, John (v. 14) reiterates that the "Word" referred to is the Son, and notes that He "became flesh" (the Incarnation). Only the Son has a body. The Word = Jesus = God.

The Bible Never Says That Jesus Is God? Wrong!

John 10:30: I and the Father are one.

Jesus' hearers, unbelieving Jews, certainly understood His intent in saying this, because they tried to stone Him, as the next verse informs us, since they didn't believe His claim, which, if untrue, would have been intolerable blasphemy. John 10:33 informs us that the unbelieving Jews tried to stone Him because (in their words) "you, being a man, make yourself God."

John 20:28: Thomas answered him, "My Lord and my God!"

This had to do with the famous Doubting Thomas incident. Thomas didn't believe Jesus had risen, so Jesus appeared for His sake and told him to touch His wounds. Then Thomas believed and said, "My Lord and my God!" If it were untrue, Jesus would have corrected him, but He didn't; He commended Thomas because he believed.

Colossians 1:19: For in him all the fulness of God was pleased to dwell.

In context, it is the Son who is being described (Col. 1:13); He is eternal (Col. 1:15, 17-18), the Creator (Col. 1:16), and the unifying principle of the universe (Col. 1:17; cf. Heb 1:3): all attributes that are true only of God. Paul makes the notion even more explicit in the next chapter:

Colossians 2:9: For in him the whole fulness of deity dwells bodily.

2 Peter 1:1: our God and Savior Jesus Christ.

St. Paul uses the same phrase in Titus 2:13 as well.

Hebrews 1:8: But of the Son he says, "Thy throne, O God, is for ever and ever, the righteous scepter is the scepter of thy kingdom."

This is a remarkable passage, in which God the Father calls His Son "God." It is a reference to the Old Testament passage, Psalm 45:6-7.

In Hebrews 1:6, God the Father also says that all the angels should worship God the Son. Worship can be rightly applied only to God, as we know from Exodus 34:14 and Deuteronomy 8:19. Yet Jesus accepted worship of Him on many occasions (e.g., Matt. 14:33; 28:9) and stated that He should be honored equally with the Father (John 5:23). In Revelation 5:8, 12-13 and Colossians 2:6-7, we find that Jesus is worshipped in *every* way that the Bible specifically describes worship of God the Father, with all the same words used (see Rev. 4:9-11; 5:13; 7:11-12; Rom. 11:33).

Jesus is omnipotent (possesses all power):

Philippians 3:20-21: the Lord Jesus Christ, who will change our lowly body to be like his glorious body, by the power which enables him even to subject all things to himself.

He's omniscient (all knowing):

Colossians 2:2-3: Christ, in whom are hid all the treasures of wisdom and knowledge.

He's omnipresent (present everywhere):

Ephesians 1:22-23: the church, which is his body, the fulness of him who fills all in all. (cf. Col. 3:11)

The Bible Never Says That Jesus Is God? Wrong!

Another astonishing passage along these lines is one in which Jesus speaks about historical events described as being done by God the Father in the Old Testament. He casually applies them to Himself (what might be called "the Divine 'I'"):

> **Matthew 23:34, 37**: Therefore I send you prophets and wise men and scribes, some of whom you will kill and crucify, and some you will scourge in your synagogues and persecute from town to town.... O Jerusalem, Jerusalem, killing the prophets and stoning those who are sent to you! How often would I have gathered your children together as a hen gathers her brood under her wings, and you would not!

Many attributes that are said to belong only to God are applied to Jesus in Scripture. God the Father said, "[B]esides me there is no savior" (Isa. 43:11; cf. 1 Tim. 4:10). Yet Jesus is called the savior of mankind in passages such as Luke 2:11 and many others.

God the Father stated, "To me every knee shall bow, every tongue shall swear" (Isa. 45:23). The same exact description is also applied to Jesus (Phil. 2:10-11).

The Bible teaches that God is judge (e.g., 1 Sam. 2:10; Ps. 50:6; Eccles. 12:14). But so is Jesus (John 5:22, 27; 9:39; Acts 10:42; 2 Tim. 4:1). Therefore He is God.

God the Father sits on His throne in heaven (1 Kings 22:19; Ps. 11:4; 47:8). Jesus is on the same throne, too (Rev. 7:17; 22:1, 3).

At every turn in the Bible, only one conclusion is possible, to make sense of all these statements, taken together as a whole: Jesus is God the Son. He is the eternal, all-powerful, all-loving, self-existent Creator God.

52

The Holy Trinity Proven from Scripture

Briefly put, the Holy Trinity is the belief that the one God subsists in Three Persons: God the Father, God the Son (Jesus, who took on flesh in the Incarnation and became man), and God the Holy Spirit. They are all God, with the same divine attributes, yet are in relationship with each other as subject and object.

It is ultimately a deep mystery, because we can't fully comprehend how three can be one. It seems to go against logic. Yet the Bible plainly teaches it, with many and varied proofs, and so we must accept the revealed doctrine in faith, bowing to the fact that God's thoughts are much higher than ours (see Isa. 55:9).

The Trinity is a classic case in which there are few "direct" proofs, but many, many deductive or indirect proofs, which can hardly be dismissed by any person who accepts the inspiration of Holy Scripture, God's revelation.

No single passage states, "The one God exists in three Persons: Father, Son, and Holy Spirit." Yet, for example, we see a verse that strongly suggests the same, with just a little deduction:

> **Matthew 28:19**: Go therefore and make disciples of all nations, baptizing them in the name of the Father and of the Son and of the Holy Spirit.

The Holy Trinity Proven from Scripture

If the Bible teaches that God (and only God) has certain characteristics, and proceeds to apply them to three Persons: called the Father, Son, and Holy Spirit, then they are all one God (since the Bible teaches there is but one: Deut. 6:4; 32:39; Isa. 43:10; 44:8; 1 Cor. 8:4-6).

In my research, I have found forty passages that mention all three Divine Persons. Here are eight of them (just one-fifth of the number I found):

Isaiah 61:1: The Spirit of the Lord GOD is upon me. (cf. Isa. 61:2; Jesus applies this to Himself in Luke 4:16-30)

Luke 3:21-22: [W]hen Jesus also had been baptized and was praying, the heaven was opened, and the Holy Spirit descended upon him in bodily form, as a dove, and a voice came from heaven, "Thou art my beloved Son; with thee I am well pleased." (cf. Matt. 3:13-17)

John 15:26: But when the Counselor comes, whom I shall send to you from the Father, even the Spirit of truth, who proceeds from the Father, he will bear witness to me. (cf. 14:26)

Acts 2:33: Being therefore exalted at the right hand of God, and having received from the Father the promise of the Holy Spirit, he has poured out this which you see and hear. (cf. Acts 7:55)

Acts 20:28: Take heed to yourselves and to all the flock, in which the Holy Spirit has made you overseers, to care for the church of God which he obtained with the blood of his own Son.

Romans 15:30: I appeal to you, brethren, by our Lord Jesus Christ and by the love of the Spirit, to strive together with me in your prayers to God on my behalf. (cf. Eph. 2:18)

1 Corinthians 6:11: justified in the name of the Lord Jesus Christ and in the Spirit of our God. (cf. 1 Pet. 1:2)

2 Corinthians 13:14: The grace of the Lord Jesus Christ and the love of God and the fellowship of the Holy Spirit be with you all.

Is the Holy Spirit directly referred to as God? Yes; here is the best single passage along those lines:

Acts 5:3-4: But Peter said, "Ananias, why has Satan filled your heart to lie to the Holy Spirit and to keep back part of the proceeds of the land?... You have not lied to men but to God."

Ananias lied to the Holy Spirit at the same time he lied to God; therefore, the Holy Spirit and God are synonymous — one and the same.

This sort of thing occurs over and over in the Bible: equivalent characteristics in many respects are applied to all three Divine Persons:

1. *Who raised Jesus from the dead?* Well, it was God the Father (Gal. 1:1; 1 Thess. 1:10); it was also Jesus Himself (John 2:19; 10:17-18); and it was the Holy Spirit (Rom. 8:11).

2. *Who gave the new covenant?* The Father (Jer. 31:33-34); Jesus (Heb. 8:1-13; 10:29; 12:24; 13:20); the Holy Spirit (Heb. 10:15-17).

3. *Who sanctifies believers?* The Father (1 Thess. 5:23); Jesus (Heb. 13:12); the Holy Spirit (1 Pet. 1:2).

The Holy Trinity Proven from Scripture

4. *Who is the creator?* The Father (Gen. 1:1; Isa. 44:24; Acts 17:24; Eph. 3:9); Jesus (John 1:3; Col. 1:16; Heb. 1:8, 10); the Holy Spirit (Job 33:4).

5. *Who indwells believers?* The Father (1 Cor. 3:16; 2 Cor. 6:16; 1 John 3:24); Jesus (John 6:56; Rom. 8:10; Eph. 3:17); the Holy Spirit (John 14:16-17; Rom. 8:9, 11; 1 Cor. 3:16). The Bible even describes this in terms of different combinations: Father and Son (John 14:23); Father and Holy Spirit (Eph. 2:21-22; 1 John 3:24); Son and Holy Spirit (Gal. 4:6).

What one Person does, the others also do in complete agreement and unity, and the Persons "interpenetrate" each other. Christian theology has 50-cent words for this: *circumincession* (Latin) and *perichoresis* (Greek).

Lots of things are very difficult to understand yet firmly believed; for starters: quantum mechanics, the physics of black holes, the nuclear fusion that occurs in the center of our sun, the "bending" of space and time (Einstein's relativity). Physical reality has turned out to be very "weird" and unpredictable. Theology is also sometimes striking, and seemingly "odd" and unfathomable. This should not surprise us at all (since God is an extraordinary Being).

Cumulative arguments based on scores of individual indications become very compelling: much as a large rope, consisting of many individual strands woven together is exceedingly strong. Such is the nature of biblical indications for the Holy Trinity. We find them at every turn. No one should be led astray into thinking that the Holy Trinity is not "biblical." Having seen the many reasonable proofs, we believe in faith.

53

Is Trinitarianism Demonstrable from Scripture Alone?

I was writing back and forth with a Protestant pastor. He said that, if he spoke on the Trinity in a Catholic environment, the Catholics in attendance would think that Protestants "got" the doctrine of the Trinity from Catholics and not from Scripture alone and that Catholics believe in it solely because the Church teaches it and not because the Bible teaches it. This was my reply:

That's not how most Catholics I know would think about it at all. We would rejoice in the truths you taught about, knowing that we hold them in common. We would be glad to learn more about a highly important subject. It wouldn't matter a hill of beans that you were a Protestant, anymore than it matters that William Lane Craig is a Protestant philosopher when he defends the Resurrection or gives his brilliant version of the Cosmological Argument. I love that stuff, and so do most sensible Catholics. We quickly forget that the source may happen to be a Protestant and rejoice in the truth presented.

Only a polemically motivated, overzealous Catholic would think in the way you have described. Now, granted, if there were some big debate about the topic, some of that might come

Is Trinitarianism Demonstrable from Scripture?

out, but even then, I think you have caricatured the Catholic position.

As an apologist, I have written on this topic, and I would never present it in such terms. It's far more complex than that. But in a nutshell, I would say: yes, the Trinity can be explicitly proven from many biblical passages (see the previous two chapters). I presuppose that it is clear and undeniable from Scripture alone.

What Catholics actually say about the authority issue with regard to the Trinity is that (much as you would say, I'm sure) human sin and false premises can cause sinful men to distort the Bible and find in it a non-Trinitarian view. We see examples all around us: Jehovah's Witnesses, Christadelphians, Mormons, and so forth. So an authoritative Church is very useful to declare things dogmatically.

It doesn't follow from that that the Trinity was *not* clear in the Bible alone without the Church. If you read the Fathers opposing the Arians, you'll see this dynamic very clearly. They argue for the Bible, but then they end the argument by appealing to the Church and apostolic tradition.

The first thing is the material element, and the second is the formal. They'll say, "The Church has always taught the Holy Trinity all the way back to the beginning; therefore it is true, because the Church is protected by the Holy Spirit, and the teaching goes back to Jesus and the apostles."

But the Arians had no such history they could produce, so they had to fall back on the Bible alone; but they distorted the Bible with bogus prooftexts that Jesus was supposedly created.

Both things are true: the Trinity is true because the Bible teaches it, and it is true because the Church has always taught it. The second is not "over" the first, as if the first has no validity in and of itself.

Proving the Catholic Faith Is Biblical

We believe exactly the same about the canon of the Bible. The Bible is what it is, independently of the Church's declaring it to be so. The books do not become inspired merely because the Church said so. They are inspired because they are God-breathed. Vatican I and Vatican II both state this.

Nevertheless, it is good to have an authoritative list of canonical books because, in fact, the Fathers disagreed somewhat on those in the early centuries, and an objective statement was necessary to avoid continuing disagreement.

You can always find people who will think illogically and not understand the teaching of the Church they are part of. In the end, you can go only by official Church teachings. But I have not found this particular thing to be the case very often, and I was a committed evangelical for thirteen years and have been a committed Catholic for almost twenty-four, and an apologist in both camps.

54

Trinitarian Baptismal Formula and "Jesus Only" Baptism

It is often argued by those who deny the Trinity (groups such as the United Pentecostal Church or so-called apostolic denominations, corresponding to their Sabellian or "Oneness" Christology); also by a few Trinitarian denominations that adopt a "Jesus only" baptismal formula, that Acts 2:38 provides us with the correct baptismal formula (i.e., the words pronounced by the person performing the sacrament). Others contend that Acts 2:38 contradicts Matthew 28:19. Some higher critics of the Bible have argued (typical of their "method") that Matthew 28:19 is a later extrapolation into the biblical text. Here is the text under consideration:

> **Acts 2:38-39**: And Peter said to them, "Repent, and be baptized every one of you in the name of Jesus Christ for the forgiveness of your sins; and you shall receive the gift of the Holy Spirit. For the promise is to you and to your children and to all that are far off, every one whom the Lord our God calls to him."

The Trinitarian baptismal formula is based on Matthew 28:19; what is called the Great Commission (an express command of Jesus):

Go therefore and make disciples of all nations, baptizing them in the name of the Father and of the Son and of the Holy Spirit.

In the context of Acts 2, the phrase "in the name of Jesus Christ" was not a liturgical formula, but a way of distinguishing Christian baptism from the baptism of John the Baptist (cf. Acts 19:1-5). Matthew 28:19 shows that awareness and acceptance of the Holy Trinity is also necessary. Hence, in context, Peter mentions the Holy Spirit: "Repent, and be baptized … and you shall receive the *gift of the Holy Spirit*." God the Father is included in the next verse as well: "For the promise is to you and to your children and to all that are far off, every one *whom the Lord our God calls to him*."

Moreover, fairly explicit Trinitarianism is present in Acts 2:32-33, in the same sermon on the Day of Pentecost:

This Jesus God raised up, and of that we all are witnesses. Being therefore exalted at the right hand of God, and having received from the Father the promise of the Holy Spirit, he has poured out this which you see and hear.

The passage in Acts 2:38 is not intended as a *formula* and doesn't record an actual baptism or the words spoken during it (because Peter is commanding baptism for all Christians, not actually performing it). In any event, to use the phrase "baptized in Jesus' name" (in a nonformulaic way) does not *theologically* contradict the Trinitarian baptismal formula.

The baptismal formula adopted by the Church in her rite and sacrament of baptism from the beginning is the one recorded in Matthew 28:19. We see this in the *Didache*, a very important apostolic writing, dated as early as A.D. 60-70, which places it

Trinitarian Baptismal Formula

earlier than even some biblical books. In this work we find the following passage (7:1):

> After the foregoing instructions, baptize in the name of the Father, and of the Son, and of the Holy Spirit, in living [running] water. If you have no living water, then baptize in other water, and if you are not able in cold, then in warm. If you have neither, pour water three times on the head, in the name of the Father, and of the Son, and of the Holy Spirit. Before baptism, let the one baptizing and the one to be baptized fast, as also any others who are able. Command the one who is to be baptized to fast beforehand for one or two days.

Many other Church fathers bear witness to the Trinitarian baptismal formula. In the Bible itself, there are many passages that associate Jesus' name (in some fashion: we are contending that it is a nonformulaic use) with baptism (Acts 8:16; 10:48; 19:1-5; 22:16; Rom. 6:3-4; 1 Cor. 1:13; 6:11; Gal. 3:27).

When Jesus gave the explicit Trinitarian formula of Matthew 28:19, Matthew, Peter, John, and the other disciples (minus Judas) were present, and Luke would surely have learned of that through these sources. We know about that because it is recorded; therefore, it (i.e., the baptismal formula) is definitely part of the apostolic deposit.

The disciples heard this with their own ears, and it had to do with one of the basic rites of the Church. They were not at liberty to change that (nor is the Church). It would have been unthinkable. That was the tradition that they had to preserve and promulgate.

The question, then, is whether the Bible verses above that mention Jesus contradict the Trinitarian formula. They do not.

Proving the Catholic Faith Is Biblical

It's not an either-or proposition. Since Peter heard what Jesus taught about the formula to be used, he would not and could not have contradicted it.

"In the name of [the Lord] Jesus Christ" is not a formula but a summation of a different idea: Jesus was the name that was revealed (Phil. 2:9-10; cf. 2 Thess. 1:12; 1 John 3:23), and He was the one whom Christians served. They healed in and by His name (Acts 3:6; 4:10, 30; 16:18), and called upon Him (1 Cor. 1:2). Moreover, Peter is *commanding* baptism for all Christians, not actually *performing* it in Acts 2:38.

Indeed, St. Paul states: "And whatever you do, in word or deed, do everything in the name of the Lord Jesus, giving thanks to God the Father through him" (Col. 3:17). Paul said he would die "for the name of the Lord Jesus" (Acts 21:13). Therefore, to use the phrase "baptized in Jesus' name" (in a nonformulaic way) does not theologically contradict the Trinitarian baptismal formula of Matthew 28:10.

A Catholic Commentary on Holy Scripture[19] comments accordingly on Acts 2:38:

> To Semites the name is the person. "Baptism in the name" means "to be, by the fact of baptism, consecrated, dedicated, subjected to someone."... Jesus has been shown to be the Messias. To join his community, to belong to him, his baptism must be received. Thus "baptism in the name of Jesus" is not a liturgical formula, but distinguishes Christian baptism from, e.g., that of John the Baptist, 19:5, or that given to proselytes. Mt 28:19 and St. Paul's

---

[19] Edited by Dom Bernard Orchard (London: Thomas Nelson and Sons, 1953).

Trinitarian Baptismal Formula

question in 19:3 show that knowledge of the Holy Trinity was necessary, and each Person is mentioned here in 38-39.

A. T. Robertson expresses the same notion:

In the Acts the full name of the Trinity does not occur in baptism as in Matthew 28:19, but this does not show that it was not used. The name of Jesus Christ is the distinctive one in Christian baptism and really involves the Father and the Spirit.... "Luke does not give the form of words used in baptism by the Apostles, but merely states the fact that they baptized those who acknowledged Jesus as Messiah or as Lord."[20]

If this is part of the reasoning employed by those who think there was a different formula in the very early Church, I think it fails by not bringing into consideration the above factors regarding how "the name of Jesus" was used and understood by the earliest Christians, in their culturally Jewish context.

---

[20] Robertson, *Word Pictures in the New Testament*, vol. 2, comment on Acts 2:38.

55

Should God the Father Be Visually Depicted in Paintings?

As long as it is understood as artistic license, God the Father may be depicted in painting. The Bible teaches that God the Father is an invisible spirit (Col. 1:15; 1 Tim. 1:17), but I think it is permissible to portray the "idea" of God the Father visually, just as the Holy Spirit was portrayed (by God's design) as a dove at Jesus' baptism (see Matt. 3:16; Mark 1:10; Luke 3:22; John 1:32).

Likewise, God the Father on several occasions in the Old Testament presented Himself visually in the form of the "Angel of the Lord" or in what are known as "theophanies" (see, e.g., Exod. 3:2-6). This being the case, paintings of God the Father, although not literal to His nature, are permissible, since the Bible permits similar representations of the Father and the Holy Spirit (neither of whom has a body or physicality).

Moreover, there is even some biblical basis for visualizing God the Father as the stereotypical old man with white hair. The prophet Daniel saw this in one of his "visions" (Dan. 7:7):

> **Daniel 7:9**: As I looked, thrones were placed and one that was ancient of days took his seat; his raiment was white as snow, and the hair of his head like pure wool;

Should God the Father Be Visually Depicted?

his throne was fiery flames, its wheels were burning fire. (cf. Rev. 1:13-15, which describes Jesus in similar fashion)

The "son of man" (the Messiah or Jesus) appeared before the Father and was given dominion over the kingdom (Dan. 7:13-14). Jesus referred to this passage and "coming on the clouds of heaven" during His trial (Matt. 26:64; cf. Mark 14:62).

56

Satan's Tempting of Jesus as a Proof of Jesus' Divinity

Matthew 4:1-7: Then Jesus was led up by the Spirit into the wilderness to be tempted by the devil. And he fasted forty days and forty nights, and afterward he was hungry. And the tempter came and said to him, "If you are the Son of God, command these stones to become loaves of bread." But he answered, "It is written, 'Man shall not live by bread alone, but by every word that proceeds from the mouth of God.'" Then the devil took him to the holy city, and set him on the pinnacle of the temple, and said to him, "If you are the Son of God, throw yourself down; for it is written, 'He will give his angels charge of you,' and 'On their hands they will bear you up, lest you strike your foot against a stone.'" Jesus said to him, "Again it is written, 'You shall not tempt the Lord your God.'" (cf. Luke 4:1-13)

In my own opinion, this passage has a double application: primarily to God the Father, but also to Jesus Himself. After all, Matthew 4:1 says He was "tempted by the devil" (cf. Matt. 4:3; Luke 4:2, 13). Matthew 4:7 is a citation of Deuteronomy 6:16.

Satan's Tempting of Jesus as a Proof of Jesus' Divinity

In the context of that passage, the Jews were tempting God to show them a miracle.

So what do we have here? The devil challenged (or tempted) Jesus to turn stones into bread (Matt. 4:3), and referred to Him (cynically and mockingly, but with knowledge) as "the Son of God."

We know from John 5:18 that in the Jewish mind, "son of God" was tantamount to being God ("This was why the Jews sought all the more to kill him, because he not only broke the sabbath but also called God his Father, making himself equal with God."). The Jews even tried to stone Jesus in one instance because He called God His Father (John 10:30-36).

Satan knew who Jesus was. James 2:19 states: "You believe that God is one; you do well. Even the demons believe—and shudder" (cf. Mark 1:24; Luke 4:34).

The Church Father Hilary of Poitiers wrote: "Thus beating down the efforts of the Devil, He professes Himself both God and Lord." This was included in the *Catena Aurea* of St. Thomas Aquinas (a commentary on Matthew that collected patristic commentary). I think it is a legitimate secondary application of the verse. Hilary thought so, too (and St. Thomas quoted him to that effect), and I suspect others could be found if we looked hard enough. Granted, I don't think it's one of the stronger arguments for the divinity of Jesus (of which there are literally hundreds) by a long shot, but it's interesting, plausible, and possible, and it doesn't appear that we can totally rule it out from what we have in the text and in cross-textual considerations.

57

Jesus' Acceptance of Praise as a Proof of His Divinity

This is, I submit, one of those innumerable proofs of the deity of Christ that are so plain (presented almost in a ho-hum fashion in Scripture, so to speak) that we can easily miss them:

> **Matthew 21:14-16**: And the blind and the lame came to him in the temple, and he healed them. But when the chief priests and the scribes saw the wonderful things that he did, and the children crying out in the temple, "Hosanna to the Son of David!" they were indignant; and they said to him, "Do you hear what these are saying?" And Jesus said to them, "Yes; have you never read, 'Out of the mouth of babes and sucklings thou hast brought perfect praise'?"

Do you see what is happening here? The "praise" (Jesus' word) is directed toward *Jesus*, but praise of this sort is to be directed only to God; hence, Jesus is God. It is made crystal clear by looking at the Old Testament citation, because what was applied to God the Father there is now applied to Jesus, and He *accepts* it:

> **Psalm 8:1-3**
> O LORD, our Lord,
> how majestic is thy name in all the earth!

Jesus' Acceptance of Praise

*Thou whose glory above the heavens is chanted
by the mouth of babes and infants . . .
When I look at thy heavens, the work of thy fingers,
the moon and the stars which thou hast established . . .*

58

Jesus Is Explicitly, Directly Called "God" (Romans 9:5)

KJV: Christ came, who is over all, God blessed for ever. Amen.

Douay-Rheims: Christ, according to the flesh, who is over all things, God blessed for ever. Amen.

NASB: the Christ according to the flesh, who is over all, God blessed forever. Amen.

This is the literal rendering of the Greek. Hence, *Young's Literal Translation* (the most literal in English) translates: "the Christ, according to the flesh, who is over all, God blessed to the ages. Amen."

Other translations bring the meaning out more explicitly:

NKJV: Christ came, who is over all, the eternally blessed God.

Knox: Christ, who rules as God over all things.

NIV: Christ, who is God over all.

Phillips: Christ who is God over all.

Jesus Is Explicitly, Directly Called "God"

Beck: Christ, who is God over everything.

I naturally (with my apologist's instinct and heartfelt orthodoxy) like these five "explicit" renderings, yet the text is slightly ambiguous, so this is not an "airtight" passage. Yet at least five translations, including one Catholic one (Knox), present this passage as an explicit proof for the divinity of Jesus, or His being directly called or addressed as "God."

This occurrence is infrequent, in any event (John 20:28; Titus 2:13; and 2 Pet. 1:1 being probably the three best instances), and often denied altogether as present in the Bible, by detractors of Trinitarian Christianity and Christology and by folks who just don't know their Bibles very well (sadly, legion).

Jesus' Agony in the Garden vs. "Be Not Anxious"

Matthew 26:37-38: And taking with him Peter and the two sons of Zebedee, he began to be sorrowful and troubled. Then he said to them, "My soul is very sorrowful, even to death; remain here, and watch with me."

Mark 14:33-34: And he took with him Peter and James and John, and began to be greatly distressed and troubled. And he said to them, "My soul is very sorrowful, even to death; remain here, and watch."

Jesus' emotions in the garden are described with the Greek words *lupeo* (sorrowful [Strong's word no. 3076]) in Matthew 26:37; and *perilupos* (exceedingly sorrowful [Strong's word no. 4036]) in Matthew 26:38 and Mark 14:34. These are neutral terms insofar as the question of sin or right and wrong are concerned. Sorrow and sadness are not sins. Jesus wept over the death of Lazarus. This is not a sin; it is being human and compassionate, and Jesus had a human nature as well as a divine nature.

Jesus' instruction to "be not anxious," on the other hand, uses a different word: *merimnao* (Strong's word no. 3309). This had to do with anxiety, worry, fear about what the future held in store.

Jesus' Agony in the Garden vs. "Be Not Anxious"

Jesus told His followers not to be anxious in, for example, the Sermon on the Mount (Matthew 6:34). It's not a case, then, of Jesus telling us not to do something, and then doing it Himself.

A similar question arises (in some skeptical minds) regarding Mary and Joseph looking for Jesus when He was twelve and not being able to find Him for a time:

> **Luke 2:48**: And when they saw him they were astonished; and his mother said to him, "Son, why have you treated us so? Behold, your father and I have been looking for you anxiously."

It comes down, again, entirely not only to definitions of words but context. Mary and Joseph were simply concerned about the welfare of their son, which is not a sin. All parents do that. The word for "anxiously" in the RSV here is a different one: *odunao* (Strong's word no. 3600). The same word ("sorrowing" in the RSV) is used when Paul's followers say farewell to him (Acts 20:37-38). No sin at all.

Even *merimnao* is not *absolutely* prohibited. Paul uses it in the sense of "caring for" (1 Cor. 7:32-34), and quite positively, in 1 Corinthians 12:25 and Philippians 2:19-20. He used the cognate *merimna* in 2 Corinthians 11:28: "anxiety for all the churches."

Jesus was urging His followers not to worry or get anxious about what what might be. That shows a lack of trust and faith. But Jesus had no *doubts* in the garden; He simply agonized over the suffering He was willingly to undergo.

Would we really expect Him to feel *otherwise*? If He didn't suffer in some sense, He wouldn't have a human nature, as He does. This is one reason we love Him so much: He is like us in almost all respects except for sin. The Bible states repeatedly (including several instances of Jesus' own words) that Jesus suffered (Matt.

16:21; 17:12; Mark 8:31; 9:12; Luke 9:22; 17:25; 22:15; 24:26, 46; Acts 3:18; 17:3; 26:23; Rom. 8:17; 2 Cor. 1:5; Phil. 3:10; Heb. 2:9-10, 18; 5:8; 9:26; 13:12; 1 Pet. 1:11; 2:21, 23; 4:1, 13; 5:1).

There is no trace in Scripture of attributing sin to Jesus. He can agonize in His human nature; that is no difficulty whatever. It is a result of the Incarnation and what He came to earth to do on our behalf.

60

Annulment Is Not Catholic Divorce

A widespread perception exists, among Protestants, secular society, our Orthodox brethren, and even too many Catholics that annulment is simply a sophisticated, "playing with words" equivalent of divorce. This is untrue. The distinction between divorce and annulment is one that is routinely made even in civil law. It is not unique to, nor was it invented by, Catholicism.

For example, the *Oxford Companion to Law* states that "Annulment of a marriage is legislative or judicial invalidation of it, as in law never having existed, as distinct from dissolution [divorce], which terminates a valid marriage."[21]

In a considerable number of scenarios, the Church recognizes that a legitimate, sacramental marriage was never present from the outset. One has to enter into marriage with a free will and full understanding of what it entails. The proverbial shotgun wedding is a classic case in which the free will of at least one party is abrogated. A person might, for example, marry someone who did not reveal that he was a practicing criminal, or someone with an unknown severe mental illness, or someone who, say

[21] *Oxford Companion to Law*, ed. D. M. Walker (Oxford, Clarendon Press, 1980), s.v. "Annulment."

(to use an extreme example for the sake of illustration), turns out to be a spy from a hostile government, or one who is already married (bigamy). All of these scenarios (and many others) are illegitimate "marriages" and nonsacramental from the start.

It's often noted that much higher rates of annulment occur today. Abuses in the process do, no doubt, take place, due to societal and peer pressure and sin and human weakness. But the prevalence of abuse (I've learned, from talking to canon lawyers) is likely far less than is often casually assumed.

It's also indisputable that more and more people have a limited understanding from the outset of what a sacramental marriage is and what it entails; hence, such "marriages" were never *sacramentally* valid in the first place. This lack of knowledge would be an altogether valid reason and explanation for greater numbers of annulments than were formerly seen. Our society's view of marriage is much weaker than in the past, with many couples having such a low view of it that they don't even seek marriage.

The Old Testament distinction between a concubine and a wife is somewhat analogous to ours between a civil and sacramental marriage — itself the foundational premise of the concept of annulment. Concubines were distinguished from wives, even multiple ones (Judges 8:30-31). God approved of sending away Hagar and her son Ishmael (Gen. 21:12), not because they were evil or disparaged by Him (see Gen. 17:20; 21:13, 17-20), but because Sarah was Abraham's wife in the full sense (akin to sacramental marriage).

Likewise, in Ezra 10:1-19, 44 (cf. Ezra 9:1-2, 14-15), many Israelites "put away" (Ezra 10:19) the "foreign women" they had married, not simply because they were foreigners, but because they caused them to become corrupted by false religions and idolatry (see, e.g., Deut. 17:17; Neh. 13:23-28). This was essentially

Annulment Is Not Catholic Divorce

an annulment, as opposed to a divorce, because these unions had a serious impediment in the eyes of God and in light of His laws. They were not in accord with what God had commanded.

If one is looking for New Testament verification of the notion of annulment, the "except for unchastity" clause of Matthew 19:9 is interpreted by Catholic commentators (and the Church fathers en masse) as a case of nonmatrimonial cohabitation as opposed to real marriage. In other words, Jesus was saying that if someone divorces his wife, he commits adultery, except in cases where he actually was *not* married in the first place. That is an annulment: straight from our Lord.

Oddly, many commentators (and individual Christians) seem to think that "unchastity" in Matthew 19:9 refers to the *adultery* of one of the marriage partners (thus allowing a permissible divorce). But the Greek word here (*porneia*) is rarely if ever translated "adultery" in the passage. The usual Greek word for "adultery" is *moicheia*.

Porneia and related cognates are *never* translated in the King James Version, for example, as "adultery," but always as "fornication" or other such terms. We also see the two Greek words distinguished from each other in the same verse (Matt. 5:19; Mark 7:21; Gal. 5:19). All of this supports the traditional and dogmatic Catholic understanding that Jesus was referring in Matthew 19:9 to something other than an adulterous affair of a truly married person.

Moreover, the "Pauline privilege" has always been accepted by the Church:

> **1 Corinthians 7:15**: But if the unbelieving partner desires to separate, let it be so; in such a case the brother or sister is not bound. For God has called us to peace.

The Church has held that a Christian is free to remarry in cases where two nonbelievers (generally unbaptized) marry, one later becomes a Christian, and the non-Christian departs. This is because the natural (or what we often call "civil") marriage was not sacramental in the first place.

Hence, St. Ambrose wrote in A.D. 385 in his letter 19:7 to Vigilius: "Since the marriage ceremony ought to be sanctified by the priestly veiling and blessing, how can that be called a marriage ceremony where there is no agreement in faith?"

Likewise, Pope St. Leo the Great, writing in 459 to Rusticus (Epistle 167:4), stated, in reference to Abraham and Hagar:

> Since the marriage tie was from the beginning so constituted as apart from the joining of the sexes to symbolize the mystic union of Christ and His Church, it is undoubted that that woman has no part in matrimony, in whose case it is shown that the mystery of marriage has not taken place.

In summary, then, annulments are recognized in civil law and have an explicit exegetical basis. Catholics need not fear close examination, nor be "ashamed" of the issue.

61

"Be Fruitful and Multiply"

Some things are so obvious that we take them for granted. We don't feel that we need to "argue" them because we casually assume that everyone knows they are true. The lyrics to an old Frank Sinatra song come to my mind: "Love and marriage go together like a horse and carriage."

But wait! This seeming commonsense "truism" has been largely lost, in terms of being the norm in our society. Today love and marriage *don't* always go together, and we see thousands of couples living together without being married. And, of course, now even marriage as solely between a man and a woman is up for question.

Marriage and procreation is another such obvious pairing that is increasingly denied today. What once was understood by virtually everyone (certainly all Christians) no longer is, and is rejected outright by more and more couples.

So we Catholics and other conscientious parents concerned with educating children in traditional morality need to go back to the basics and cite inspired Holy Scripture to reinforce basic moral truths — sort of like learning our ABCs all over again.

The Bible is quite clear on this point, and — as in many cases, including even the very existence of God — *assumes* its truth, so much so, that it doesn't bother to explain *why* it's true. In fact, the very *first* command to man recorded in the Bible is "Be fruitful and multiply" (Gen. 1:28).

We might also note (taking into account common complaints and misunderstandings about Catholic teaching) that what the Church calls the *unitive* purpose of marriage is also alluded to early on in Genesis, where God says: "It is not good that the man should be alone; I will make him a helper fit for him" (Gen. 2:18). Marriage is not *only* for procreation; nor does it consist only of pleasure and companionship, but *both*. Yet procreation is the fundamental purpose and essence of marriage (and the relations within it). The notion of fruitfulness and multiplying is repeatedly presented as a blessing in the Bible (Gen. 9:1, 7; 35:11; Ps. 107:38; Isa. 48:18-19; Jer. 29:6; 30:19-20; 33:22; Ezek. 36:10-12; Dan. 3:35-36; Bar. 2:34). The ultimate cause of this increasing is *God*, not man and his choices, although man indeed "works together" with God, always enabled by His grace (cf. 1 Cor. 3:9-10; 15:10; 2 Cor. 6:1; Phil. 2:13):

> **Genesis 28:3**: *God Almighty bless you and make you fruitful and multiply you.*
>
> **Deuteronomy 7:13-14**: *[H]e will love you, bless you, and multiply you; he will also bless the fruit of your body and the fruit of your ground, your grain and your wine and your oil, the increase of your cattle and the young of your flock, in the land which he swore to your fathers to give you. You shall be blessed above all peoples; there shall not be male or female barren among you, or among your cattle.*
>
> **Psalm 105:24**: *And the* LORD *made his people very fruitful, and made them stronger than their foes.* (cf. Ps. 115:14)

"Be Fruitful and Multiply"

This is the natural order of things. We've come from that to a strange place where three or more children are considered too many. My wife and I ran into two nice ladies at our local Highland Games, and we mentioned that we had four children. One of them immediately shot back with, "Oh, you must be *Catholic*." I didn't think fast enough at the time. Instead of smiling sheepishly and saying, "Yeah," I should have replied, "We have four children because we're *married*." That would have been much more interesting and could quite possibly have led to a fruitful discussion (no pun intended).

It's too bad that we don't also have a popular song with the line: "Lots o' kids and marriage: go together like a horse and carriage," but no doubt that would be scorned just as the coupling of "love and marriage" or "husband and wife" is.

The world is turned upside down: in the wrong direction. The ugly fruit of secularism is apparent. Thus, our task is to present traditional moral teaching to our children and anyone else, when the topic comes up, and to explain why we believe as we do: to defend what used to be patently obvious to one and all.

62

God Blesses Parents with Children

We can learn a lot from words, especially if we go back to the Latin roots of many of our English words. All Christians are familiar with the notion of God as the Creator. He made all things from nothing (theologians describe this with the wonderful Latin phrase *creatio ex nihilo*).

The word *procreate* has an obvious linguistic and conceptual connection with creation. Mothers and fathers don't create their children all by themselves but are vessels used by God, who has brought all the wonderful processes of reproduction into being. Parents participate in the unspeakable privilege of the creation of a new child and work together with God, as so often in Scripture. Yet the child's soul is a supernatural creation from God and has nothing to do with biology.

The problem today, in our massively contraceptive culture, is that we have forgotten that God is Creator and the primary participant and ultimate cause in procreation as well: the bearing of children, as a function of His providence, whereby He has a hand in all things, for His eternal purposes; all things working together for good (Rom. 8:28), for those who love Him.

Somehow we fallen persons too often think it is all *our* doing when a child is conceived, and nothing of God's—as if natural

God Blesses Parents with Children

processes were all that is involved in children's being conceived and born. We're trained by our secular culture to think in terms of both individual control and the primacy of nature, over against supernature, or grace (insofar as the latter is acknowledged at all).

The Bible takes a far different view, and the phrase "opened her womb" is used in reference to God with regard to both Leah (Gen. 29:31) and Rachel (Gen. 30:22). It's not just a trite observation on the level, say, of a popular greeting card. It's a profound truth. Real cause and effect is in play. Other passages teach the same thing:

> **Joshua 24:3-4**: Then I took your father Abraham from beyond the River and led him through all the land of Canaan, and made his offspring many. I gave him Isaac; and to Isaac I gave Jacob and Esau.
>
> **Ruth 4:13**: So Boaz took Ruth and she became his wife ... and the LORD gave her conception, and she bore a son.

Moreover, Scripture describes God as the primary Creator throughout the process of conception and childbirth: "Thy hands fashioned and made me" (Job 10:8); "Thou didst clothe me with skin and flesh, and knit me together with bones and sinews" (Job 10:11); "In his hand is the life of every living thing" (Job 12:10); "[D]id not one fashion us in the womb?" (Job 31:15); [T]he LORD who made you, who formed you from the womb" (Isa. 44:2; cf. Isa. 44:24).

Granted, the parents and natural processes are also causes. But we mustn't *remove God from the equation,* or in effect, tie His hands when He would will that a child be born, and we overrule Him, so to speak. This is the evil in contraception, or what is known as the "contralife will." When we are open to life, we freely work together with God, His will, and His providence in our lives, for our good and that of our children.

It doesn't follow that every Catholic couple *must* have a dozen children or as many as is humanly possible. The Church allows spacing of children (by means of Natural Family Planning [NFP], not contraception) and limiting of children in circumstances that warrant it (health or financial reasons). What is *not* allowed is the deliberate separation of the procreative function of marriage from the unitive (pleasurable) function, so that the latter is sought without the intrinsic connection to the former.

God knew what that separation would bring about in society, and we see the sad, tragic fruit of this dangerous point of view all around us. Our task is not just to live out the Catholic life ethic consistently, but also to understand the positive (not merely "negative") underlying reasons for it, and to share them with others.

The many biblical passages about children (especially, *many* of them) being a great blessing suggest procreation as the central purpose of marriage (certainly the very opposite of a contraceptive outlook):

Genesis 17:16: I will bless her, and she shall be a mother of nations; kings of peoples shall come from her.

Genesis 33:5: The children whom God has graciously given your servant.

1 Chronicles 25:5: All these were the sons of Heman the king's seer, according to the promise of God to exalt him; for God had given Heman fourteen sons and three daughters.

God Blesses Parents with Children

Psalm 127:3-5: Lo, sons are a heritage from the LORD, the fruit of the womb a reward. Like arrows in the hand of a warrior are the sons of one's youth. Happy is the man who has his quiver full of them!

We ignore God's inspired Word and the godly counsel of Holy Mother Church at our peril. The God who created us knows what will make us joyful, fulfilled, and at peace, as His disciples. God the Father knows best!

63

Onan's Sin and Punishment

The constant tradition of the Catholic Church has been to prohibit artificial contraception. In this the Catholic Church seems to be almost alone today. Yet, historically speaking, all Christian groups opposed contraception altogether until the Anglicans decided in 1930 to allow it for "hard cases" (how sadly *familiar* that reasoning sounds!).

It's often thought that the Catholic reasoning behind the prohibition stems from a sort of "anti-sex" or "anti-pleasure" or prudish motivation. The Catholic Church supposedly doesn't "like" sex, so she requires priests and nuns to be celibate and seeks to take as much pleasure as possible out of the wondrous divine gift of sexuality. This is untrue, but suffice it for now to say that the relevant biblical arguments have been used by Protestants as well, and stand on their own.

This scriptural basis is perhaps seen most clearly in the passage concerning the sin of Onan:

> **Genesis 38:9-10**: [W]hen he went in to his brother's wife he spilled the semen on the ground, lest he should give offspring to his brother. And what he did was displeasing in the sight of the LORD, and he slew him also.

Onan's Sin and Punishment

The reasoning often used to overcome the force of the passage is to say that Onan was punished by God (with death) for disobeying the "levirate law," whereby a brother of a dead husband was to take his sister-in-law as his wife and have children with her (Deut. 25:5-10). But that can't apply in this case (or any other) because the law allows the brother to refuse and recommends that the one who does so suffer only public humiliation. Thus we find in Deuteronomy 25:9 that a sister-in-law so refused should "spit in his face," but there is no mention of any wrath from God, let alone the death penalty.

Moreover, the passage that teaches about the levirate law (Deut. 25:5-10) is directly from God, as part of the covenant and the Law received by Moses on Mount Sinai and proclaimed to all of Israel (see Deut. 5:1-5; 29:1, 12). God Himself did *not* say that the punishment for disobeying the levirate law was death (in the place where it would be expected if it were true).

If refusal alone was not grounds to be killed by God or by capital punishment issued by his fellows, there must have been something in the *way* Onan refused that was the cause. This was the "withdrawal method," a form of contraception (probably the one most used throughout history, because it requires no devices or potions). Therefore, Onan was killed for doing that, which means (we can reasonably conclude) that God didn't approve of it.

The levirate law itself confirms the central point on which the moral objection to contraception is based: the evil of separating sex from procreation. It is precisely because the primary purpose of marriage is procreation that the levirate law was present in the first place. If one married, they were to have sexual relations, which was (foremost) for the purpose of having children.

If a husband died with no children, it was so important to continue his name with offspring that God commanded the man's brother to take his wife after he died. But Onan tried to separate sex from procreation. He wanted all the pleasure but not the responsibility of perpetuating his brother's family. He possessed the "contraceptive mentality" that is rampant today, even (sadly) among otherwise traditional, committed Christians.

Fr. Brian Harrison wrote an excellent article in which he examined the passage in great exegetical depth, with incorporation of pertinent cross-texting. He states:

> As is well-known, Scripture always refers to licit (married) intercourse only in an oblique way: "going in to" one's wife, (i.e., entering her tent or bedchamber, cf. vv. 8 and 9 in the Genesis text cited above, as well as Gen. 6:4; II Sam. 16:22; I Chron. 23:7) or "knowing" one's spouse (e.g., Gen. 4:17; Luke 1:34). When the language becomes somewhat more explicit — "lying with" someone, or "uncovering [his/her] nakedness" — the reference is without exception to sinful, shameful sexual acts. And apart from the verse we are considering, the Bible's only fully explicit mention of a genital act (the voluntary emission of seed) is in a prophetical and allegorical context wherein Israel's infidelity to Yahweh is being denounced scathingly in terms of the shameless lust of a harlot (Ez. 23:20).[22]

The evil of the contraceptive act stems from its willful, unnatural separation of what God intended to be together. It violates natural law. Onan tried the "middle way" (and the "modern

---

[22] Brian W. Harrison, "The Sin of Onan Revisited," *Living Tradition*, no. 67, November 1996, http://www.rtforum.org/lt/lt67.html.

Onan's Sin and Punishment

way") of having sex but willfully separating procreation from it. This was the sin, and it's why God killed him.

Obviously, God is not immediately punishing or judging in this fashion today (or if so, only in the very rarest of cases), but the point of the Old Testament was to make clear what was right and wrong, and to punish evil swiftly and decisively. Therefore, we learn from this passage that contraception is quite gravely sinful and forbidden; and this general principle of morality didn't change with the arrival of the new covenant and Christianity.

64

Reply to an Attack against NFP and Spacing of Children

A "traditionalist" argued the following things (all false, and number 4 is a distortion and contrary to fact):

1. Women must be open to having an unlimited number of children.

2. Married couples cannot decide to limit this number for any reason.

3. Married couples cannot decide to space children for any reason.

4. Bl. Pope Paul VI made a "drastic change" in Catholic tradition by making the purpose of marriage happiness of the couple rather than procreation.

5. Bl. Pope Paul VI's reasons given in [the 1968 encyclical] *Humanae Vitae* for limiting and spacing children are wrong and come from "Protestant" reasoning: against Catholic tradition.

6. Natural Family Planning (NFP) is no different from artificial contraception and is, therefore, evil. It is a

Reply to an Attack against NFP

corruption of traditional teaching, not a development of it.

Following is my reply to all these serious errors and distortions of what the Church teaches and has taught:

Humanae Vitae is infallible teaching, and NFP is a legitimate, consistent development of the ban on contraception. Spacing children for the right reasons is perfectly acceptable and Catholic. The unitive function of marriage has always been part of it. To deny that is to feed into stereotypes that Catholics are antisex and antipleasure and that all that women are good for is to be baby-making machines.

Similar thinking of this sort leads to genital mutilation of women (or "female circumcision"), which still occurs today in many cultures. Women are not supposed to have any pleasure in sex, right (which would be shocking news to the writer of the Song of Solomon)?

Spacing can be done for health, financial, or emotional reasons (as *Humanae Vitae* discusses). Bl. Pope Paul VI wrote:

> In relation to physical, economic, psychological, and social conditions, responsible parenthood is exercised, either by the deliberate and generous decision to raise a numerous family, or by the decision, made for grave motives and with due respect for the moral law, to avoid for the time being, or even for an indeterminate period, a new birth. (section 10)

Take my family's case, for example (to see how this works out in a real-life scenario). God has blessed my wife and me with four wonderful children. We did practice NFP. Why? Well, we have never had much money (given that I am an apologist, a profession that is not thought much of), and that is a legitimate consideration (having fifteen children and a fairly low income is not a wise life choice).

But there were also serious health reasons. My wife, Judy, has had six miscarriages, and very difficult pregnancies (the last one required several months of bed rest).

Moreover, there were emotional difficulties, with *extremely* serious postpartum depression after our second child (who had colic for a good year, so that her sleep was severely disrupted, and I couldn't help much since my wife nursed the children and I had a driving job and so couldn't be up all night either).

These are all perfectly legitimate reasons to exercise NFP. And it's no different in essence from the following biblical passage:

> **1 Corinthians 7:4-5**: For the wife does not rule over her own body, but the husband does; likewise the husband does not rule over his own body, but the wife does. Do not refuse one another except perhaps by agreement for a season, that you may devote yourselves to prayer; but then come together again, lest Satan tempt you through lack of self-control.

NFP is, in effect, one such "season." The couple abstains during fertile periods, for good and permissible reasons (assuming these are present, in good conscience; NFP is also itself abused if used wrongly for illegitimate motives). This is fundamentally different from contraception, because the couple who practices NFP accepts the natural order of things and natural law by not having sex during fertile periods.

Contraception eliminates the possibility of conception (during fertile periods), thus violating God's law, by not willing a

Reply to an Attack against NFP

child who might be, if sexual relations occur. In other words, it is immoral to engage in sexual relations when a woman is fertile and deliberately thwart what might be a conception. That is not being open to life. NFP involves no such contralife will, because it counsels abstinence during fertile periods (for the right reasons).

To understand these issues better, I highly recommend *The Teaching of "Humanae Vitae": A Defense*, by John C. Ford. S.J., Germain Grisez, Joseph Boyle, John Finnis, and William E. May. In the chapter "Every Marital Act Ought to Be Open to New Life: Toward a Clearer Understanding," the authors say:

> There is a real and very important difference between not wanting to have a baby, which is common to both [1. contraception] and [2. the noncontraceptive use of NFP], and not wanting the baby one might have, which is true of (1) but not of (2).[23]

---

[23] John C. Ford. S.J., Germain Grisez, Joseph Boyle, John Finnis, and William E. May, *The Teaching of "Humanae Vitae": A Defense* (San Francisco: Ignatius Press, 1988), 89.

Contraception, Murder, and the Contralife Will

1. One can murder a person after he is conceived.

2. One can deliberately prevent any chance of a person being conceived, through contraceptive means or mentality, or both.

Both statements are contralife or anti-life. Obviously, the second isn't technically murder, but it accomplishes the same goal: it is against the person that may be conceived if intercourse were not divorced from its deepest, procreative purpose:

1. Contraception is a deliberate act of preventing the conception of Person X who would have been conceived had the couple been open to new life.

2. Therefore, the goal or intention is to obliterate the (earthly) existence of Person X.

3. That is also the goal of a murder: to obliterate the (earthly) existence of Person X.

4. Therefore, in the deepest sense, contraception and murder are alike, and evil.

Contraception, Murder, and the Contralife Will

5. Contraception, however, takes it a step further and disallows even the *beginning* of Person X, who might have been or would have been conceived, *were it not* for contraception.

6. Thus, contraception obliterates not only the earthly existence of Person X but any existence whatsoever of the person, in terms of having an eternal soul.

7. In that sense, contraception is even more anti-life than murder is.

8. Therefore, in a qualified, specific sense, contraception can almost be said to be as heinous and wicked as (and philosophically equal to) murder.

Number 6 is mainly looking back (analogically) to murder, which obliterates a person's earthly existence. Contraception goes beyond that insofar as it denies even a soul or a spiritual existence to a person who might have been. It goes beyond the body to the soul.

It *does* make sense to talk of potential persons, based on God's omniscience, and middle knowledge, as part of that omniscience. God knows what might have been, in all possible situations: things that would have happened, given different variables, as results of actual events. This is not mere speculation. For those who accept the inspiration of Scripture, it's demonstrated:

Matthew 11:21: "Woe to you, Chorazin! woe to you, Bethsaida! for if the mighty works done in you had been done in Tyre and Sidon, they would have repented long ago in sackcloth and ashes."

Note that God has certain knowledge of what the inhabitants of Tyre and Sidon *would* have done, had conditions been different (if they had seen the works of Jesus and heard His message). God knew that. Yet it was not an actual event; only a potential or conditional one.

Here's another:

> **1 Corinthians 2:7-8**: But we impart a secret and hidden wisdom of God, which God decreed before the ages for our glorification. None of the rulers of this age understood this; for if they had, *they would* not *have crucified the Lord of glory.*

And a third:

> **Jeremiah 23:21-22**: "I did not send the prophets, yet they ran; I did not speak to them, yet they prophesied. But if they had stood in my council, then they would have proclaimed my words to my people, and they would have turned them from their evil way, and from the evil of their doings."

Now, with this in mind, let's look at what happens in contraception and its relation to potential or possible persons who never do actually exist:

1. A couple engages in lovemaking, using contraception (for the sake of argument and simplicity, let's assume it is 100 percent effective in preventing conception).

2. Had they not done so, there would have been some chance (depending on fertility and the right conditions) for a person to be conceived. We shall call such potential persons X, Y, and Z.

Contraception, Murder, and the Contralife Will

3. X, Y, and Z might have actually existed, had they not been prevented from coming into existence by a contralife will that wishes to separate the deepest purpose of sexuality (procreation) from sexual acts.

4. God in His perfect will may very well have intended that a person be brought into existence by a particular sexual act. But the contracepting couple have made that perfect will of God impossible by contraception. They want to separate the act from its deepest and most beautiful meaning.

Another way of putting it is this:

1. X, Y, and Z are those persons who would have *actually* come into existence had contraception been absent during lovemaking (so many times, by so many people). Because of contraception, they do *not* exist.

2. Therefore, X, Y, and Z have been prevented from having an existence at all—even in terms of having a soul—by contraception. And this is contralife.

3. God actually *knows* who these persons would have been; what their lives would have been like. And He would have had a plan and a vocation for each of them. We know He knows this because of His middle knowledge (*scientia media*), as shown in Matthew 11:21 and two other passages.

4. Moreover, we know it from Jeremiah 1:5:
    Before I formed you in the womb I knew you, and before you were born I consecrated you; I appointed you a prophet to the nations.

5. God knew this about an actual person, Jeremiah. But He would also know it about potential persons, on the same basis that He knew what the inhabitants of Tyre and Sidon would have done, under different conditions.

Abstinence from sex is not contralife. No contralife will or act occurs by simply abstaining, nor by, for example, having sex during infertile periods or after menopause or in the case of a person being infertile through no deliberate intention of his own. None of that is contralife, nor is mere spacing of children, provided that natural law is upheld, and the couple abstains during fertile periods.

The contralife will lies in not being open to a possible conception: to new life, as a result of the sexual act. It's contralife and evil to prevent deliberately any life from being conceived, while simultaneously enjoying the pleasure of sexuality. This is what is perverse and against natural law.

And it is easily shown to be so by analogy. Suppose we have a person who eats only for pleasure and not for nutrition at all. He wants to eat Butterfinger bars and donuts all day long, and for dessert it's lemon meringue pie and cotton candy. You get the point. Now what do we instinctively think of such a person? We think he is a *nut*, that he is unbalanced, acting like a spoiled and very immature child. And why is that? Because we know that food is not just for pleasure; it is primarily for nutrition.

The same could be said (in a little different way) about the folks in the old Roman vomitoria. For them, food was for pleasure, only to be regurgitated up after being devoured and enjoyed. Likewise, anorexia and bulimia are seen as abnormal and psychologically disordered.

Contraception, Murder, and the Contralife Will

God gave us taste buds, too, but the two things must be kept in balance. So we think a person is weird if he cares only about the taste of food and not at all about its nutritional value.

And we think the same of the extreme health food nut who seems to separate all pleasure from food and eats bark and grubs and other such goodies, because they have a high protein or fiber content. We think that person is as odd as the junk-food junkie.

Yet in secular society and among Christians who have bought secularism and bought into the sexual revolution to some extent, sexuality that separates procreation from the pleasure of sexuality is not viewed as abnormal or disordered at all. That's just, well, personal freedom and the "right" to engage in unlimited pleasurable activity.

Perhaps someone can explain to me why sexuality is viewed that way, while eating food is not.

66

Does the Bible Condemn Homosexual Acts?

MARRIAGE AND FAMILY[24]

The Catholic Church is wrong to condemn homosexuality, because homosexuality is natural.

No church has any right to tell people what to do with their own bodies.

Initial reply

The Bible clearly condemns homosexual acts as intrinsically, gravely sinful. Desperate attempts to explain away this prohibition are futile; the Bible is too clear.

Extensive reply

For those who believe that the Bible is God's inspired word, this issue is easily resolved. Catholics and other Christians didn't make this rule; God did. But if one denies that the Bible is inspired, then, of course, none of the following proof texts will matter:

[24] This chapter is also written in the format of my book *The One-Minute Apologist*.

Does the Bible Condemn Homosexual Acts?

Leviticus 20:13: If a man lies with a male as with a woman, both of them have committed an abomination; they shall be put to death, their blood is upon them. (cf. Lev. 18:22)

Judges 19:22-23: [B]ehold, the men of the city, base fellows, beset the house round about, beating on the door; and they said to the old man, the master of the house, "Bring out the man who came into your house, that we may know him." And the man, the master of the house, went out to them and said to them, "No, my brethren, do not act so wickedly; seeing that this man has come into my house, do not do this vile thing."

1 Kings 14:24: [A]nd there were also male cult prostitutes in the land. They did according to all the abominations of the nations which the LORD drove out before the people of Israel. (cf. 1 Kings 15:12; 22:46; Deut. 23:17; 2 Kings 23:7)

1 Timothy 1:8-11: Now we know that the law is good, if any one uses it lawfully, understanding this, that the law is not laid down for the just but for the lawless and disobedient, for the ungodly and sinners, for the unholy and profane, for murderers of fathers and murderers of mothers, for manslayers, immoral persons, sodomites, kidnapers, liars, perjurers, and whatever else is contrary to sound doctrine, in accordance with the glorious gospel of the blessed God with which I have been entrusted.

Jude 7: [J]ust as Sodom and Gomorrah and the surrounding cities, which likewise acted immorally and indulged in unnatural lust, serve as an example by undergoing a punishment of eternal fire. (cf. Gen. 19:4-7 and 2 Pet. 2:4-10; the latter describes the behavior of the Sodomites as not merely violent rape but "licentiousness of the wicked" and "lust of defiling passion")

Objection
What is condemned in the Bible is selfish, abusive sex (of any kind), not homosexuality per se, which is simply a natural desire of some people. We know much more now about genes and psychology than they did in biblical times.

Reply to Objection
God doesn't change. If He states that something is sinful and never permissible, that prohibition applies at all times. Secondly, it isn't true that the Bible condemns only homosexual rape and not such acts by mutual consent. All the passages above, except Judges 19:22-23 and 1 Timothy 1:8-11 condemn consensual homosexual acts. Jude 7 mentions "unnatural lust" and 2 Peter 2:4-10 states similarly. Therefore, this objection collapses. As for the desire itself, Catholics don't believe it is inherently sinful, as long as it isn't acted upon (*Catechism of the Catholic Church*, nos. 2358-2359), just as heterosexual lust, fornication, and adultery must be rejected in the will, by God's grace, in order to avoid sin. Everyone has more than enough temptations to resist and overcome.

St. Paul in Romans 1 makes an explicit argument against homosexuality, as an unnatural practice; he also presents a similar argument in 1 Corinthians 6:12-20, by stating that excessive appetite for sex (and also food?) amounts to being "enslaved" (1 Cor. 6:12). There is a created reality and natural order beyond mere physical pleasure, which must not be violated. Certain things are wrong by their very nature. Sex outside of marriage — whether

Does the Bible Condemn Homosexual Acts?

heterosexual or homosexual—belongs to that category (1 Cor. 6:18-20). Again, he casually assumes that sodomy is intrinsically wrong in 1 Timothy 1:8-11.

> The disciples were not told why (in terms of efficient cause) the man was born blind (Jn. 9:1-3): only the final cause, that the works of God should be made manifest in him. This suggests that in homosexuality, as in every other tribulation, those works can be made manifest: i.e., that every disability conceals a vocation.... The homosexual has to accept sexual abstinence just as the poor man has to forego otherwise lawful pleasures because he would be unjust to his wife and children if he took them.[25]

---

[25] C. S. Lewis, letter of May 14, 1954, in Sheldon Vanauken, *A Severe Mercy* (New York: Bantam Books, 1979), 146, abbreviations removed.

67

St. Paul's Argument from Nature against Homosexual Acts

Romans 1:26-27: For this reason God gave them up to dishonorable passions. Their women exchanged natural relations for unnatural, and the men likewise gave up natural relations with women and were consumed with passion for one another, men committing shameless acts with men and receiving in their own persons the due penalty for their error.

St. Paul mentions "dishonorable passions." He then gives an example of what he calls "dishonorable": "Their women exchanged natural relations for unnatural." Paul is saying, then, that there is such a thing as "natural [sexual] relations" and its contrary, "unnatural" sexual relations. This brings it down to the matter of natural law and God's created order, and all that that entails. Some things are natural, some are not. So far, I have merely followed the syntactical and grammatical logic of the passage (at least in its translation). I don't think anything I have stated thus far could be argued differently, regardless of one's stance on homosexuality.

What follows in the next verse is clearly related to what came before it: "and the men likewise gave up natural relations

St. Paul's Argument against Homosexual Acts

with women and were consumed with passion for one another." This is very clear-cut. The word *likewise* inescapably implies that the men, too, have abandoned "natural relations" for "unnatural" ones (since it is an analogy). In other words, the contrast is between natural and unnatural, and also between heterosexual and homosexual sex. Paul is not merely saying that the "dishonorable passions" are what is sinful, but rather the very *concept* and *practice* of homosexual relations, which goes against nature.

Since it is "unnatural" for men to be (sexually) with men, and women with women, according to the apostle (and God, since the Bible is God-breathed), Paul describes the sexual acts as "shameless" and in "error." There is no qualification here for things such as rape or promiscuity or uncommitted, manipulative sex (the frequent desperate eisegesis of those who already believe the Bible is neutral on the issue). St. Paul makes an argument from nature. He is saying that the very notion of homosexuality is disordered and unnatural.

Romans 1:18-32 is a sort of primitive teleological argument (or argument from design). Paul implies sins against nature in Romans 1:24: "the dishonoring of their bodies among themselves." Idolatry is condemned in Romans 1:25: "they ... worshiped and served the creature rather than the Creator ..."

Immoral sex of any sort (heterosexual or homosexual) amounts to a worship of the physical body as an object apart from the whole person who possesses it, and in defiance of the lifelong commitment within which moral sex is protected and placed in the proper context of whole love relationships with whole people (not just genitals), for a whole lifetime.

As mentioned in the last chapter, St. Paul makes a similar argument from nature (but a bit more sophisticated and theological) in 1 Corinthians 6:12-20, by stating that excessive appetite for sex amounts to being "enslaved" (6:12). He exclaims:

> **1 Corinthians 6:16**: Do you not know that he who joins himself to a prostitute becomes one body with her? For, as it is written, "The two shall become one flesh."

In other words, there is an ontological, created reality and natural order beyond mere physical pleasure, which must not be violated. Certain things are wrong by their very nature. Sex outside of marriage (either heterosexual or homosexual) belongs in that category. Paul continues:

> **1 Corinthians 6:18-20**: Shun immorality. Every other sin which a man commits is outside the body; but the immoral man sins against his own body. Do you not know that your body is a temple of the Holy Spirit within you, which you have from God? You are not your own; you were bought with a price. So glorify God in your body.

Heterosexual fornication and adultery are just as sinful, wicked, reprehensible, and unnatural as homosexual sex. These sexual sins violate the bounds of proper sex between males and females as God intended it, within a lifelong monogamous commitment of marriage. The same physical act that is right and proper and beautiful in one situation (in marriage) becomes sinful in another (with a prostitute or with someone other than one's spouse).

Homosexuality also violates this boundary, but it goes a step further and violates the created order of sex itself, which God intended for male and female (this is self-evident in the complementary physiology of the reproductive organs, and in the result of conception).

St. Paul's Argument against Homosexual Acts

One might say that fornication is an "ontological" sin against the moral "concept" of marriage, while homosexual sex sins both against the purpose of sex and the ontological, metaphysical, and spiritual (even physical) nature of sex itself. God's laws and natural law are spurned and scorned.

On the other hand, Paul seems to teach that *all* forms of sexual immorality are a sin against nature and against the Holy Spirit within us. Something bad actually happens in the very real spiritual realm. We become joined with the harlot. We sin against ourselves and our own bodies as well. We violate the temple of God (ourselves, if we are Christians, since the Holy Spirit dwells in us).

I don't see how this could be any clearer than it is. The assertion by radical homosexual exegetes that traditional Christians are distorting the Bible's teaching (whether it is inspired and preserved properly or not) and not presenting it properly is groundless. The Bible, as it reads, is indisputably opposed to homosexual acts as a sin against nature, God, and one's own body. It's all right there in Romans 1:26-27.

The Prohibition against Premarital Sex

The prohibition against premarital sex is not at all obscure in the Bible. For example, the standard reference work, *Vine's Expository Dictionary* states:

> Fornication, Fornicator: is used (a) of "illicit sexual intercourse," in Jhn 8:41; Act 15:20, 29; 21:25; 1Cr 5:1; 6:13, 18; 2Cr 12:21; Gal 5:19; Eph 5:3; Col 3:5; 1Th 4:3; Rev 2:21; 9:21; in the plural in 1Cr 7:2; in Mat 5:32; 19:9 it stands for, or includes, adultery; it is distinguished from it in Mat 15:19; Mar 7:21.

Of many other arguments that could be made, from a variety of different contexts and words used, I would note the "one flesh" motif:

> **Matthew 19:4-6**: He answered, "Have you not read that he who made them from the beginning made them male and female, and said, 'For this reason a man shall leave his father and mother and be joined to his wife, and the two shall become one flesh'? So they are no longer two but one flesh. What therefore God has joined together, let not man put asunder." (cf. Mark 10:8)

The Prohibition against Premarital Sex

This is obviously a reference to intercourse, so that becoming "one flesh" is clearly morally done after being married, not before. St. Paul expands the argument and ties it in with the notion of the Church and Christ:

> **Ephesians 5:28-33**: Even so husbands should love their wives as their own bodies. He who loves his wife loves himself. For no man ever hates his own flesh, but nourishes and cherishes it, as Christ does the church, because we are members of his body. "For this reason a man shall leave his father and mother and be joined to his wife, and the two shall become one flesh." This mystery is a profound one, and I am saying that it refers to Christ and the church; however, let each one of you love his wife as himself, and let the wife see that she respects her husband.

The husband loves his wife because he is one flesh with her, just as Christ and His Church are one. This presupposes that sexuality is proper only within marriage. Thus, St. Paul offers a contrast of unlawful sexuality elsewhere, by noting how utterly immoral and improper in the Christian scheme of things, sexual union is outside of marriage:

> **1 Corinthians 6:9, 11, 15-20**: Do you not know that the unrighteous will not inherit the kingdom of God? Do not be deceived; neither the immoral, nor idolaters, nor adulterers, nor sexual perverts.... And such were some of you. But you were washed, you were sanctified, you were justified in the name of the Lord Jesus Christ and in the Spirit of our God.... Do you not know that your bodies are members of Christ? Shall I therefore take the members of Christ and make them members of

a prostitute? Never! Do you not know that he who joins himself to a prostitute becomes one body with her? For, as it is written, "The two shall become one flesh." But he who is united to the Lord becomes one spirit with him. Shun immorality. Every other sin which a man commits is outside the body; but the immoral man sins against his own body. Do you not know that your body is a temple of the Holy Spirit within you, which you have from God? You are not your own; you were bought with a price. So glorify God in your body.

Again, quite clearly, premarital sex is immoral, and not just when a prostitute is involved, but any unmarried woman and man. It's not fashionable to say this today (and certainly not "sensitive" or delicate), but so what? People sometimes need to be jolted into reality. We must preach against sin from the rooftops. Christianity was never about being trendy and fashionable. It's a narrow road, and part of Christianity has always been "waiting until marriage."

Just because we are in the aftermath of a disastrous sexual revolution and because cohabitation is now ultrafashionable as a new "norm" (i.e., "Everyone else is doing it, so why don't we?") doesn't change that fact. Truth is truth, and right and wrong are what they are, and are so eternally.

The zeitgeist will continue to bring disaster: personal and societal. There is a reason we have myriad broken homes today. Putting the cart before the horse doesn't work. With otherwise "serious" Christians (although I would debate even that) fornicating by the millions, we need to have as strong a message as we can against it, lest they ruin their lives, like millions before who wanted to deny Christian moral teaching.

The Prohibition against Premarital Sex

There are many biblical passages forbidding premarital and extramarital sex — whenever "fornication" or "licentiousness" or "immorality" or "sexual immorality" or "sexual vice" (various translations) are mentioned. To deny this is like saying, "There is no verse that says, 'The Holy Trinity is God in three persons.'" Sure, but there are hundreds of passages that, all taken together, teach the Holy Trinity, which is why all Christians have believed in that doctrine. A few heretical cults and sects deny it and claim that the Bible never teaches it.

No passage says, "Original Sin affects the entire human race." There isn't nearly as much in the Bible (as with, for example, the virgin birth) about that topic, but more than enough to establish that it is true, which is why, again, all Christian groups have accepted it, save a few fringe, semi-heretical groups such as Churches of Christ.

The problem, I submit, is not the unclearness of Scripture but rather the unwillingness to accept a difficult teaching and to counter worldly teachings and fashionable trends (post sexual revolution) in order to hold to biblical and traditional Christian teaching. In research projects I have undertaken over the past thirty-three years, I've always found that Scripture is pretty clear.

I maintain that the prohibition against sex outside of marriage is quite sufficiently clear in Scripture. It requires just a little bit of study. For anyone familiar with the Bible, it's manifestly there, which is precisely why this was the uniform teaching among evangelical Protestants until we came to this place now where it is fashionable in those circles to question it.

There are lots of clear passages condemning homosexual acts, yet lots and lots of Christians continue to butcher the Bible to find support for that. Young people are becoming overwhelmingly in favor of "gay marriage."

Proving the Catholic Faith Is Biblical

There is no support for female clergy or priests in the Bible, and much about an all-male priesthood, but does that matter? No. These two things are fashionable, so it doesn't matter a hill of beans what Scripture actually says, or what tradition and history have held.

There's plenty in the Bible about not murdering and not sacrificing children (I've collected it myself), yet almost all Protestant denominations have espoused abortion. Again, it was fashionable, so it was done despite what the Bible taught.

The same dynamic is present in this debate. I don't think most people who want to water down the true teaching are simply carnal monsters. It's complex, as with all human motivation. We understand the drives (believe me, I do). People interpret in a framework. They sort of "go with the flow." This is what is ominous today. As the zeitgeist goes more and more against moral tradition, people jump on the bandwagon. Scripture becomes irrelevant.

And if we Catholics agree that Scripture is so radically unclear on these issues, we help support the tendency, even though we oppose it. We "condemn" those who will *not* consult Catholic tradition and the Church to believing the trends and the fad, by saying no one can arrive at the truth in the Bible by itself on the issue of premarital sex.

69

Does 1 Corinthians Sanction Premarital Sex?

I ran across a guy who thought he had proven the permissibility of premarital sex in the Bible. He considered the passage he produced especially compelling for his position in the King James Version. Here it is:

> **1 Corinthians 7:36-38**: But if any man think that he behaveth himself uncomely toward his virgin, if she pass the flower of her age, and need so require, let him do what he will, he sinneth not: let them marry. Nevertheless he that standeth stedfast in his heart, having no necessity, but hath power over his own will, and hath so decreed in his heart that he will keep his virgin, doeth well. So then he that *giveth her in marriage* doeth well; but he that *giveth her not in marriage* doeth better.

Let's look very closely at the passage in context, and with consideration of the original Greek, and see if the apostle Paul explicitly sanctions premarital sexuality, as this person claimed.

The passage is not even talking about a man and his future bride (betrothed, engaged, or at least seriously in love). Paul is referring, rather, to a *father* and his *daughter*, in the context of a culture where marriages were usually arranged by the parents or at least took place with their permission and consent.

The key is the phrase "giveth her in marriage"—which makes no sense in terms of the relation of a man and future wife. It is the father who "gives in marriage." We use this terminology even today in the wedding ceremony. So something is awry here, at least in *some* translations. If indeed the passage is about a father and daughter, rather than an engaged couple, everything changes.

One must understand what refers to what in the passage. Paul is saying that a father who gives his daughter in marriage does well; if he does not, it is even better. It is a "good and better" contrast, such as Paul makes earlier in the chapter regarding the higher path of remaining celibate and single (1 Cor. 7:1, 7-8, 25-27, 32-35, 38) versus getting married (also a very good thing: 1 Cor. 7:2, 9, 28, 38).

Paul's main point in all cases is that everyone should live as he is called by God to do: whether married or single (1 Cor. 7:7, 17, 20, 24). But the single state is to be celibate, not involving the sin of fornication (1 Cor. 7:2, 9; cf. 1 Cor. 6:9, 15-20).

So why the confusion in some translations as to whether this "virgin" is a betrothed future wife of a man or his *daughter*? The original Greek might explain some of that. The literal phrase in 1 Corinthians 7:37 is "*terein ten heautou parthenon*," translated by A. T. Robertson in his *Word Pictures in the New Testament* as "to keep his own virgin daughter." That this verse refers to a virgin daughter of a man is verified by the *Expository Dictionary of New Testament Words*, by W. E. Vine (listed under "Virgin/Parthenos"):

> Those concerning whom the Apostle Paul gives instructions regarding marriage, 1 Cor 7:25, 28, 34; in 1 Cor 7:36-38, the subject passes to that of "virgin daughters"

Does 1 Corinthians Sanction Premarital Sex?

(RV), which almost certainly formed one of the subjects upon which the church at Corinth sent for instructions from the Apostle; one difficulty was relative to the discredit which might be brought upon a father (or guardian), if he allowed his daughter or ward to grow old unmarried. The interpretation that this passage refers to a man and woman already in some kind of relation by way of a spiritual marriage and living together in a vow of virginity and celibacy, is untenable if only in view of the phraseology of the passage.

Joseph H. Thayer's *Greek-English Lexicon of the New Testament* concurs (Strong's word no. 3933): "one's marriageable daughter, 1 Co. vii. 36 sqq."[26]

What about the business of "giving the daughter"? According to Robertson:

> Paul commends the father who gives his daughter in marriage (*gamizei*). This verb *gamizw* has not been found outside the N.T. See on Matthew 22:30.

Matthew 22:30 reads:

> For in the resurrection they neither marry nor are given in marriage, but are like angels in heaven. (cf. Mark 12:25; Luke 20:34-35)

Note also the related passages:

> **Luke 17:27**: They ate, they drank, they married, they were given in marriage, until the day when Noah entered

---

[26] Joseph H. Thayer, *Greek-English Lexicon of the New Testament* (Grand Rapids, MI: Baker Book House, 1977), 489.

the ark, and the flood came and destroyed them all. (cf. Matt. 24:38)

This is the same notion as in 1 Corinthians 7:38. Note the contrast between "marry" and "given in marriage." These are different concepts. The first refers to the man and wife, as subject; the second to the father "giving" his daughter (away) in marriage.

The Greek word in Matthew 22:30, Luke 17:27, and 1 Corinthians 7:38 is *ekgamizo* (Strong's word no. 1547), from the root *gamos* (Strong's word no. 1062), "marry." Likewise, in Mark 12:25 it is *gamisko* (Strong's word no. 1061), "given in marriage." And Luke 20:34-35 uses the cognate *ekgamisto* (Strong's word no. 1548). Thayer's lexicon confirms the meanings of all these:

> *to give* a daughter *in marriage*: 1 Co. vii. 38 ... Mt. xxii. 30 ... Mk. xii. 25; Lk. xvii. 27; xx. 35 ... (p. 109, under no. 1060a)

> *to give away ... in marriage*: a daughter, 1 Co. vii. 38 ... Mt. xxiv. 38 ... Pass. *to marry, to be given in marriage*, Mt. xxii. 30 ... ; Lk. xvii. 27 ... (p. 193, under no. 1547)

So we know what the basic meaning of the passage is now, and it has nothing even to do with sanctioned sexual intercourse of betrothed couples. It has to do, in point of fact, with parental permission or arrangement of marriage: father to daughter.

I submit that the lexicons are very clear that an unmarried daughter is being referred to here and that the phrase "given in marriage" is particularly decisive for this position.

Further arguments from general context confirm my argument. For example:

1 Corinthians 7:1-2: Now concerning the matters about which you wrote. It is well for a man not to touch

Does 1 Corinthians Sanction Premarital Sex?

a woman. But because of the temptation to immorality, each man should have his own wife and each woman her own husband.

Paul here clearly, I think, recommends marriage as the *resolution* of the problem of sexual temptation. Marriage is the place wherein sexuality is morally consummated and the natural desires channeled properly, in the overall safety of a commitment. The same dynamic occurs seven verses later:

1 Corinthians 7:9: But if they cannot exercise self-control, they should marry. For it is better to marry than to be aflame with passion.

Paul presupposes that (sexual) self-control is the norm and the goal. Failing that, the solution is to marry, not to indulge *anyway*, regardless of marriage, as if there is nothing wrong with that.

70

Thoughts on Women's Ordination

I love the fact that in my Catholic tradition, Mary, Mother of God the Son, is the very highest and holiest creature and that we have Doctors of the Church who are women (St. Teresa of Ávila, St. Thérèse of Lisieux, and St. Catherine of Siena).

No women priests? I say: so what? Different roles for different folks. Lots of other roles and functions. If God had wanted women priests He would have had a woman (or maybe six of them) — it seems quite obvious to me — among His twelve apostles. The fact that He didn't is surely highly significant.

What is the "context" of Jesus' having all male apostles? The culture of the time? Jesus wasn't reluctant to puncture sacred cows. If He wanted to have women priests and pastors, He surely would have modeled that in His disciples.

The same Paul who referred to "no male or female in Christ" also casually stated that "a bishop must be above reproach, the husband of one wife" (1 Tim. 3:2) and "Let deacons be the husband of one wife" (1 Tim 3:12). He didn't say, "A bishop must be above reproach, the husband of one wife, or the wife of one husband."

He assumes without question that it is men only. Are we to say that his teaching regarding offices in the Church was culturally

Thoughts on Women's Ordination

relative? That would have all kinds of massive implications for all kinds of things. Paul's teaching could be used to justify just about anything.

But I would deny that the restriction of priesthood to men is a matter of some screaming "inequality" in the first place. It has to do, rather, with God-ordained vocation differentiation. I can't give birth to children. I don't go around complaining about that. It's the way God made things, so I accept it. It's the same with this issue. But because it is an "ontologically spiritual" thing and not a more obvious and undeniable physical thing, it's controversial.

Any woman (in the Catholic tradition — look at St. Catherine — and I think in most, if not all, Protestant traditions) can go out and preach on the streets and evangelize all she likes. She can care for the poor; she can lead Bible studies and prayer meetings. She can do a host of things. And in fact many women do so in actuality. No one is stopping them.

All of that is different from being a priest or a pastor and presiding over the Holy Eucharist. For us Catholics, and for Orthodox, being a priest or a pastor is not merely being a good preacher or a great Bible student or a prayer warrior. It inherently involves supernatural sacramentalism: the power to preside over the miracle of the Eucharist, to grant absolution, et cetera. He directly represents Jesus Christ (*alter Christus*), and Jesus was a man.

The Bible fundamentally contradicts the notion of women's ordination. My examples of all male apostles and Paul's assumption of male bishops and elders are two examples of that. Here are two more:

1 Timothy 3:1: If any one aspires to the office of bishop, *he* desires a noble task.

Titus 1:7: For a bishop, as God's steward, must be blameless; *he* must not be arrogant.

It's fine to have a personal opinion, but the Christian's task is to harmonize such opinions with the scriptural data. It's impossible to do that (I humbly and respectfully submit) on this issue, and not because it is an argument from silence, but because it flatly contradicts passages such as the above.

Then the advocate has a huge problem of how to interpret Paul and Jesus consistently, within any interpretive grid. The Bible is not a wax nose, to be molded at will. It teaches things that can't be dismissed merely because it is faddish and fashionable in a given *zeitgeist* to deny biblical teachings.

More power to women who teach and do all kinds of ministries. I'm deeply devoted to the Blessed Virgin Mary and *love* many female saints in the Catholic tradition.

71

Philosophical Defense of the Necessity of Hell

I think we oftentimes project onto God thoughts of our own. Some people, for instance, reduce hell to some kind of petty revenge on God's part or His desire to torture people who disagree with Him. I don't think any of this is true. I wrote in one of my debates with an agnostic:

> Those who go to hell do so of their own free will, by their own free choice, having rejected the God, whose existence and nature is "clearly seen" by all (Romans 1). For the life of me, I don't understand why this should be so objectionable: God allows free creatures to reject Him and even spend eternity without Him if they so desire. Would you rather have Him force you to go to heaven rather than give you the freedom to choose heaven or hell as your ultimate destination? In any event, the existence of hell is no proof whatsoever that God is evil. It proves (almost more than anything else) that men are free.

It's not that God forces people to follow Him but that they don't *want* to follow Him, often because of misconceptions about what it means to follow God as a disciple.

Proving the Catholic Faith Is Biblical

Once we die, we enter into a timeless eternity, which cannot be other than what it is. Therefore, once we grant that there are moral distinctions to be made in this life, between good and evil, and we grant that there is a good God, it seems rather straightforward that the concept of divine justice would make it absolutely necessary for there to be a rather definite and compelling cosmic justice and weighing of the facts of what a person has done and believed in this life.

The necessity of judgment is apparent from the human analogy of laws and judges. When we do bad things, there are consequences. And often, they are irreversible. If we murder a person, that person is gone from the earth forever. The act had a consequence that to us, from the earthly, temporal perspective, is final. If we get drunk and ride a motorcycle and crash and have to lose an arm or a leg or suffer brain damage, those things are irreversible. The dumb behavior had definite consequences. A price had to be paid.

This is simply reality. By analogy, if (as I would strongly contend) the dumbest thing a person can do is reject and disbelieve in God, or in His goodness and mercy, then we would expect that there would be some extremely severe consequences to this in the long run.

Since souls are eternal by nature, that consequence is an unending place or state that is separate from God, and we have no remote conception now of how horrible it is. And to end in hell is entirely our fault, not God's. So why would anyone in effect "try God" for the existence of hell, since no one ever had to go there in the first place? It's like blaming a judge, who gives the sentence, for the existence of a penitentiary. Does that make any sense? Yet this is essentially what people do by finding hell objectionable and somehow a thing that casts aspersions on God's character.

Philosophical Defense of the Necessity of Hell

God the Father has provided a way for any man to be saved who desires to. He has made the way of salvation available through the death of His Son Jesus, who is in fact God, the second Person of the Holy Trinity. Catholicism isn't Calvinism; it doesn't teach that God predestines people to hell. I think that view (double predestination) does indeed lay God open to the charge of cruelty and arbitrariness and injustice.

Catholicism and Arminian Protestantism and Orthodoxy (which constitute the vast majority of Christians now and at all times throughout Christian history) reject this. When it is seen that people choose hell of their own free will and that God allows them to go there if they insist, that takes the "blame" off God, in my opinion. There is a strong sense in which it is absurd even to blame God for it, just as men habitually blame God for every evil: including ones that are the fault of man altogether (things such as the Holocaust or unjust laws or wars).

One who questions hell and the justice of it has to step back and ask himself: "On what *basis* do I find an eternal state apart from God nonsensical or implausible or impossible?" This entails a necessary examination of anthropology: From a theological perspective: what is man? Of what does he consist? Does he have a soul; what is that, and is it temporal, or does it have no end? Is there such a thing as sin? If so, how does God judge it, and what are its consequences? Is there such a thing as Original Sin, or the Fall, sufficiently serious enough in its rebelliousness and wrongdoing to require in the nature of things justice and punishment from the God against whom we have rebelled? Is this corporate, involving the whole human race (as the Bible clearly teaches)?

On what possible basis can one conclude that an eternal existence apart from God, of creatures who have expressly rejected this God, is an a priori impossible or unjust or implausible state of affairs?

To me it's rather simple: we are creatures who will exist from this point into the future. We will never have an end to our existence. We're like a ray in geometry: with a beginning but no end. We can be with God in eternity after we die or without Him. The choice is ours. No one has to go to hell if he will simply believe in God and follow Him, enabled by His grace to do so. These things are essentially matters of faith, part of revelation. But they are also able to be defended by many analogies to human experience and felt internal conceptions of morality and justice.

It cannot be proven that there is no such thing as atemporality. Even the laws of physics after Einstein make it rather difficult to prove. Therefore, if there is an existence outside of time or beyond time or in other dimensions, then those who have chosen certain paths will be present in this state either happily or unhappily, just as they will live on in this state in basically one condition or the other, in the deepest depths of their heart and soul.

Let's examine each of the alternative choices, to see if it makes more sense than an eternal hellfire (and heaven):

1. God chooses to annihilate people rather than having them be eternal creatures (i.e., from the time of their origin, not absolutely, like God, who has no beginning or end).

We reason, based in part on the revelation about the existence of both eternity and souls, that souls too are included in the class of things that cannot be otherwise: that they are what they are (in terms of duration) by *nature*. They are unending, just as a ray in geometry is unending. They simply keep going

Philosophical Defense of the Necessity of Hell

indefinitely, analogous to rays of light that will travel throughout the universe without end.

We might not understand it, but is it *inconceivable*? No, not at all. I see nothing implausible or unreasonable at all in the notion. And if we accept this and also some law of justice that applies to all sentient beings with moral responsibility, we arrive at the Christian notion of heaven and hell as final destination places or conditions.

2. God chooses to annihilate the ones who aren't worthy of salvation (this is the Jehovah's Witness and Christadelphian belief).

This is certainly possible, but it is contrary to biblical revelation, and it has the characteristic of "metaphysical asymmetry." If saved souls live forever, then it would seem to follow that damned souls would also, not that they would be annihilated, because in both cases, human souls are involved, and souls have the characteristic of being either temporary or endless. So it would seem to make a lot more sense that either all souls are annihilated or none (in order to have one consistent definition of a soul), but not one class only.

3. God chooses not to judge anyone at all. The evil as well as the good all end up the same. There is no "cosmic justice."

This would make the world a meaningless place, where there are no consequences of good or evil actions. That is far more horrible than the state of affairs in which good, saved people are eternally happy and bad, damned ones eternally miserable. Instead, we can commit any evil whatever and not expect any undesirable consequences for our actions. That would make God worse than the worst person imaginable. He would become evil Himself, as well as a weakling and the furthest thing from omnipotent.

4. God saves everyone.

This is also logically possible, but the problem is that it makes mincemeat of human free will, and it makes moral behavior meaningless. And, of course, it is utterly contrary to biblical revelation, if a person believes in that by faith.

5. God predestines all to hell no matter what they do or believe (the flip side of number 4).

Since this is a variation of number 4, it is subject to the same replies. We conclude, then, that the Christian scenario of heaven and hell makes (philosophically) far more sense (considered apart from revelation) than any of the alternatives.

Why do disbelievers in hell have this notion that God must work *eternally* to redeem souls? He is under no such obligation. He only has to give every person an adequate chance to believe in Him or reject Him, and we believe as Christians, based on revelation, that He more than amply does that in this lifetime.

Critics of hell presuppose that what God does to redeem a stray soul is never enough, but then we're back to blaming God again for the rebel, rather than placing the blame with the rebel, which is where it belongs. This makes no sense. We always want to blame God for everything. It's a sort of "cosmic blame shifting." We never want to blame evil, rebellious man for anything. He's always a poor, pitiful victim, and it's always God, God, God who is supposedly at fault for not having done enough.

Do we blame a parent when he does absolutely everything he should to train and provide for a child, yet the child goes astray in the exercise of his free will? Is it the parent's fault (at least in terms of primary responsibility) or the child's?

God could either give us a free will or create us as robots who followed His commands. Would we rather be robots? Once free

Philosophical Defense of the Necessity of Hell

will is granted, it makes sense to speak of good and bad eternal destinations.

To use our legal system analogy again: the judge says that a person can be paroled, given a few (not at all impossible) conditions. This is legal "mercy." But the prisoner fails to abide by these, and so he doesn't gain parole. Now, in the thinking of those who don't like hell and want to blame God for it, the one to blame for this is the parole officer or judge, because He didn't exercise enough mercy and should have forgiven the prisoner an infinite amount of times for all his violations.

In my thinking, the prisoner is at fault, not the judge, because the judge exercised clemency and mercy, and the prisoner in his stupidity failed to do the few things he had to do to receive this gracious gift.

The Church has not ruled out a possible salvation right after death. We simply don't know much about it, from revelation alone. But there is no concept of a "long" time after death or souls going from hell to heaven. Those in purgatory are saved. It is inevitable that they will be in heaven in due course. That's entirely different from the reprobate in hell.

God doesn't judge as men do—outwardly only. He knows the secrets of our hearts, so that He judges justly and fairly. No one will be sent to hell for lacking sufficient knowledge (Rom. 2:15-16).

I believe in a perfectly merciful, loving, and just God. I don't lose one second's sleep wondering about whether His judgment of souls is fair or not. *Of course it is.* Jesus reveals the nature of God and His love.

72

The Stupidity of the Devil

Satan was silly enough actually to think that he could entice Jesus to sin and diversion from His ministry. He was too ignorant in his evil irrationality to know that his scheme was doomed to failure from the beginning. We give the devil too much credit. He is an idiot and simpleton as well as a "bad guy."

I say he's stupid. How else should we describe a creature who was present with God as His highest angel, yet chose to give that up and rebel? I can think of nothing dumber and more ridiculous. The biblical definition of a fool (see, e.g., Ps. 53:1; Prov. 10:8; 12:15; 14:16; 28:26; Gal. 3:1-3) is one who has rebelled against God and who has a contempt for righteousness. In other words, I'm using *stupid* as synonymous with *foolish* or *ludicrous*, not with reference to mere intellectual capability only.

Craftiness or cleverness is not at all incompatible with monumental stupidity. Stalin and Hitler possessed both qualities in abundance. Hitler made very basic military errors, such as trying to fight two major fronts (east and west) at the same time, and attacking Russia as winter approached (the same grave mistake that Napoleon had made some 125 years earlier).

In 1942, the same year that the great apologist C. S. Lewis wrote *The Screwtape Letters*, he also wrote *A Preface to Paradise*

The Stupidity of the Devil

Lost (on John Milton's seventeenth-century epic poem on the devil and angels). In that work Lewis wrote:

> It is a mistake to demand that Satan ... should be able to rant and posture through the whole universe without, sooner or later, awaking the comic spirit.... At that precise point where Satan ... meets something real, laughter *must* arise, just as steam must when water meets fire ... and mere Christianity commits every Christian to believing that "the Devil is (in the long run) an ass." ... What we see in Satan is the horrible co-existence of a subtle and incessant intellectual activity with an incapacity to understand anything. This doom he has brought upon himself; in order to avoid seeing one thing he has, almost voluntarily, incapacitated himself from seeing at all.... He says, "Evil be thou my good" (which includes "Nonsense be thou my sense") and his prayer is granted.[27]

This sounds to me exactly like a simpleton and a fool. Nothing is dumber and more foolish and absurd than rebellion against God. The very definition of *fool* in the Bible is a person who either doesn't believe in God or doesn't follow Him as his master. I don't care how high the devil's IQ is! What good is it, seeing where he will end up? *Stupidity*, as I use it, includes a moral judgment. I'm not just using it to denote mere lack of knowledge or analytical ability. This is the biblical perspective on wisdom and knowledge.

I don't think it takes a rocket scientist to deduce that the penalty for continued rebellion against God was bound to be

---

[27]C. S. Lewis, *A Preface to Paradise Lost* (London: Oxford University Press, 1942), 95, 99.

extremely severe. Satan should have recognized that his estate was far less glorious than what he had in heaven with God. But evil is irrational by its very nature. People (and demons) who have lowered themselves want nothing more than to drag others down with them.

Our culture defines intelligence strictly in terms of IQ and the number of big words mastered and college degrees, to the neglect of moral, spiritual, and prudential elements. I much prefer the terms *knowledge* (*gnosis*) and *wisdom* (*sophia*), as I think these are the more biblical (i.e., culturally Hebrew/Jewish) categories of classification.

The devil thinks, but he doesn't "understand." He may be smart in terms of brain power, but he is a fool. His moral decisions have led to nonsense.

73

Demonic Possession or Epilepsy?

Matthew 17:15, 18: "Lord, have mercy on my son, for he is an epileptic and he suffers terribly; for often he falls into the fire, and often into the water." ... And Jesus rebuked him, and the demon came out of him, and the boy was cured instantly.

This is interesting, since it implies that epilepsy is caused by a demon, whereas we know that it has natural causes. This translation and many others (as we shall see) insinuate that it is the equivalent of demonic possession. For example, the Moffatt, 20th Century, and Weymouth versions have "epileptic" here, while KJV, Rheims, and Young's Literal have "lunatic[k]."

The older translations got it right, I think. But *lunatic* is a very unfashionable word. Of course, it is derived from observable patterns of behavior change based on the lunar cycle, which actually has some basis (we know that the moon affects the ocean tides as well). I would argue, then, that the older and more literal (and Catholic) translations are more consistent with both biblical and scientific thinking, while those that select *epileptic* here are less coherent on both scores.

Proving the Catholic Faith Is Biblical

The Greek word in question is *seleniazomai* (Strong's word no. 4583). *Strong's Concordance* defines it as "crazy; lunatic." *Thayer's Lexicon* does mention "epileptic," stating that it was influenced by the moon. But that is more evidence of natural cause, which is different from demonic cause, and in this instance, a demon was cast out.

A. T. Robertson's *Word Pictures in the New Testament* wants to have it both ways:

> Epileptic ... Literally, "moonstruck," "lunatic." The symptoms of epilepsy were supposed to be aggravated by the changes of the moon (cf. John 4:24).

Vincent's Word Studies also curiously omits mention that a demon was cast out, curing this boy:

> Is lunatic (σεληνιάζεται)
> Rev., epileptic. The A. V. preserves the etymology of the word (σελήνη, the moon) but lunatic conveys to us the idea of demented; while the Rev. epileptic gives the true character of the disease, yet does not tell us the fact contained in the Greek word, that epilepsy was supposed to be affected by the changes of the moon. See on Matthew 4:24.[28]

Vine's Expository Dictionary states similarly. All these standard sources can be read online. The famous commentator Matthew

---

[28] "A.V." refers to "Authorised Version" of the Bible; more popularly known as the King James Bible of 1611. "Rev." refers to the "Revised Version of the A.V., which came out in 1881 (New Testament) and 1885 (Old Testament). It became more or less obsolete with the advent of the Revised Standard Version (1946/1952). Marvin Vincent's *Word Studies in the New Testament* was published in 1887.

Demonic Possession or Epilepsy?

Henry (Presbyterian) offers a fascinating (and, in my opinion, superior) "mixed" view:

> The nature of this child's disease was very sad; he was lunatic and sore vexed. A lunatic is properly one whose distemper lies in the brain, and returns with the change of the moon. The devil, by the divine permission, either caused this distemper, or at least concurred with it, to heighten and aggravate it. The child had the falling-sickness, and the hand of Satan was in it; by it he tormented then, and made it much more grievous than ordinarily it is. Those whom Satan got possession of, he afflicted by those diseases of the body which do most affect the mind; for it is the soul that he aims to do mischief to.

Catholic Commentary (Orchard, 1953), likewise, calls the boy a "possessed epileptic" (I suppose he could have had two problems simultaneously). I was curious about other translations:

- *Slunatic*: KJV, Rheims, Young's Literal, NASB, Phillips, Jerusalem, NAB, Confraternity, Knox
- *epileptic* or *epilepsy*: RSV, Moffatt, 20th Century, Weymouth, NEB, REB, NIV, NRSV, ASV, NKJV, Amplified, Williams, Beck, Goodspeed, Wuest, Barclay, Lamsa
- *subject to fits*: Kleist and Lilly

The pattern, then, is older Bibles and Catholic Bibles using *lunatic* and Protestant and more recent Bibles using *epileptic*. The exceptions are Phillips and the NASB: Protestant versions from the 1950s and '60s. I prefer *lunatic*: on the basis that it is closer to the notion of "demon possessed" than *epileptic* is.

74

The Reality of Hell

The Catholic Church teaches that our fate is sealed at (or very soon after) death, and this is why it is so important to "die a good death." God can give much grace near the end, but once we die, the chances are done with. We are either saved or damned. Universalism is not possible under Catholic, Orthodox, or Protestant assumptions and the Bible's teaching.

As for a conditional hell and so forth, I don't buy it, based on Scripture, tradition, and reason. The Athanasian Creed declares: "But those who have done evil will go into eternal fire." The Fourth Lateran Council (1215) stated: "Those [the rejected] will receive a perpetual punishment with the devil." The councils of Lyons and Florence taught that the souls of the damned are punished with unequal punishment. The *Catechism* teaches the reality of an eternal hell for the reprobate who reject God (nos. 1033-1037, 1861).

Catholics are, therefore, not at liberty to reject this doctrine. It's a dogma of the Church. If it weren't true, there wouldn't be so many warnings in the Bible to avoid this horrible destiny. What sense does it make for a governor to warn everyone about the horrors of prison, when he intends to pardon everyone and send them on a vacation in Hawaii from the beginning?

The Reality of Hell

There are many unmistakable biblical teachings concerning hell. To give one example that is sufficient in and of itself, consider the judgment scene of Matthew 25:31-46. Jesus Himself says to the damned: "Depart from me, you cursed, into the eternal fire prepared for the devil and his angels" (Matt. 25:41). Matthew 25:46 summarizes: "And they will go away into eternal punishment, but the righteous into eternal life."

Now, if someone wants to do away with an eternal hell, the problem here is that the same word is used to describe the duration of both heaven and hell: *aionios* (eternal, everlasting). It is used in several places to describe eternal punishment (Matt. 18:8; 25:41,46, Mark 3:29, 2 Thess. 1:9; Heb. 6:2; Jude 7).

Case closed. One has to either accept this or deny that Scripture is inspired and infallible revelation. One believes these things in faith, but they are not contrary to reason at all. Philosophical and moral objections to hell are another thing entirely, too. It may be highly difficult to comprehend, like many things of God, but it is clearly taught in revelation, so the Christian must accept it and have faith that God knows what He is doing and is merciful and just (as we see in the life of Jesus, the Passion, and His death for us on the Cross).

Again, if no men go to hell, why is so much of the New Testament devoted to warning men not to end up there by virtue of their rejection of God? Why would the Church tell us that all mortal sins place us in potential danger of hellfire when, in fact, that never occurs because no men actually end up in hell?

That makes no sense at all. It seems to me that if universalism were in fact the true state of affairs and that all men end up in heaven, then we would be informed of this in the Bible, as it is a wonderful truth. Instead, God plays a sort of game by scaring us half to death with all this business about hell and fire and torture and all, and then no one goes there anyway except the devil and his demons.

I find that as silly and implausible as a parent who constantly scares his children with threats of punishment, but never follows through with any of it. Just as the child would not believe the parent when they make such claims, after a few years of that, I wouldn't trust God's word, either, if He acted in such a weird, arbitrary fashion with us, involving virtual deception.

Matthew 25 is clearly not an instance of a conditional prophecy (such as Nineveh or Sodom and Gomorrah, or many such prophecies given to the Israelites, contingent on their obedience to the Law). It is a description, rather, by Jesus Himself, of what *will* happen at the judgment, not what "might" happen, or only one scenario, or in terms of "*if* you do this, you'll be saved; if not, you'll be damned."

Jesus describes a scene that will actually happen. He *will* come again (Matt. 25:31). He *will* (not "may") sit and judge all the nations and separate them as sheep and goats (Matt. 25:32). He *will* say to the damned: "Depart from me, you cursed, into the eternal fire prepared for the devil and his angels" (Matt. 25:41).

This is a fact of history that God already knows, even though it is future to us. Therefore, there *will* be people in hell. It's undeniable, unarguable (if one accepts Scripture). The only "conditional" here is whether a person will accept the plain teaching of Scripture.

The following passage explicitly states that certain people are damned and undergoing eternal punishment:

Jude 7: just as Sodom and Gomorrah and the surrounding cities, which likewise acted immorally and indulged

The Reality of Hell

in unnatural lust, serve as an example by undergoing a punishment of eternal fire.

By direct implication (Jude 5, considered in context), God also sent to hell the disobedient Hebrews in the wilderness (see Exod. 32:15-35). Exodus 15:33 refers to God's blotting people out of His "book" (cf. Rev. 3:5). These people are damned! Nothing anywhere in the Bible suggests that they are given some chance to avoid their fate.

In fact, in Revelation 13:8 we learn that some people's names have "not been written before the foundation of the world in the book of life of the Lamb that was slain" (cf. Rev. 17:8). Again, by cross-referencing in this manner, the conclusion is unavoidable:

1. There is such a thing as a "book of life" that lists the elect and the saved.

2. Some people's names are not listed there or can be "blotted out." Revelation 21:27 informs us that no one who is not written in this book can enter heaven.

3. Therefore, those people are damned (and this is directly, expressly, explicitly stated in Revelation 20:11-15).

4. Therefore, there are people in hell (these same people), because hell is described as the place of eternal punishment and separation from God.

5. The people of "Sodom and Gomorrah and the surrounding cities" are literally described as "undergoing a punishment of eternal fire."

6. The disobedient Hebrews in the wilderness are placed in the same category, and by cross-referencing to Exodus we again encounter the concept of the "book of life." So are those described in Revelation 20.11-15.

7. Ergo, the proposition: "people are definitely in hell" is undeniably affirmed in Scripture in general terms (the above and Matthew 25) and in specific terms (Jude 5-7).

Another fairly direct proof that there are people in hell is all those folks of whom it is said that they will not inherit the kingdom of God, or heaven:

1. Many Jews who have ceased to believe, sufficient unto salvation. It is specifically stated that they "will be thrown into the outer darkness" (Matt. 8:11-12).

2. The evil who are compared to bad fish in a catch. The angels *will* (not "may") "throw them into the furnace of fire" (Matt. 13:47-50).

3. Jesus said it was "hard for a rich man to enter the kingdom of heaven" (Matt. 19:23-24). Thus it stands to reason that many will *not* inherit heaven.

4. In the parable of the wedding feast, the man "who had no wedding garment" is "cast into the outer darkness." Jesus ends by saying, "many are called, but few are chosen" (Matt. 22:1-14).

5. Those who aren't "born anew" cannot see the kingdom (John 3:3).

6. Various categories of unrepentant sinners "will *not* inherit the kingdom of God" (1 Cor. 6:9-10 and Gal. 5:19-21; Eph. 5:5).

7. "Flesh and blood cannot inherit the kingdom of God." Unregenerate natural man without supernatural assistance and God's grace (1 Cor. 15:49-50).

The Reality of Hell

At the judgment at the great white throne, people were judged on the basis of "the book of life." It is obviously a matter of differential eternal destinies. "Death and Hades were thrown into the lake of fire" (Rev. 20:14). This clearly means that those in Hades (who hadn't been taken to heaven with the advent of Jesus) were now sentenced to hell.

The same applies to Matthew 25. If it is not describing actual events of the end times, it is a false prophecy (from Jesus Himself), trying to get across the notion that people will be damned by the express proclamation of our Lord, when in fact no such thing happens because all are saved. This does violence to Scripture and the plain meaning of the English language.

My challenge to universalists or annihilationists or those who deny an eternal hell is to tell me how Jesus would speak if indeed many men went to hell. I contend that He could hardly be any clearer than He already is. People don't accept it because they have an objection to hell and eternal damnation before they even approach the text, and so they eisegete—that is, they arbitrarily read their own preferences into the text.

If all, in fact, are to be saved, God would certainly make that crystal-clear, precisely because the doctrine of hell is so troubling to many, even those who fully accept it; and the passages noted above would either be entirely absent or would read vastly differently.

75

A Perfect God Creating an Imperfect World

What God creates is already less perfect than He is, just by the fact that it is *created*, whereas He is eternal and uncreated. So, for example, men are not omniscient or omnipotent or omnipresent, as God is. They're not absolutely perfect, and indeed cannot be, since there is only one God, who is perfect and self-existent, needing nothing whatsoever. Men are limited in knowledge and ability. This is what caused the Fall: Adam and Eve did what was not best for them, for lack of knowledge and faith in God.

The fallacy in the atheist premise and attempted "difficulty" for Christianity is that paradise was perfect. It wasn't perfect, because it wasn't God. It was without sin at first and was "good," but the limitations were there, causing the rebellion and the Fall.

The basic problem is that there is (1) God and (2) everything else that is not God. What is not God can never be equal to God, and even God can't make it so. God can't create a second God, because that wouldn't be God: not being eternal and self-existent.

All (in this alleged conundrum) depends on what *perfect* means. God created the angels, and they had a choice to sin or not to sin. Most of them chose not to and have remained that way ever since. Some, including Satan, chose to rebel against God. Most of what causes pain and suffering is because of man's

A Perfect God Creating an Imperfect World

sin, and the rest is due to the fixed nature of the physical world (if you fall off a building and strike a hard surface, you get hurt or even die). That's not God's fault at all. If we have physical matter, and some of it is sharp or hard, sometimes people will get hurt.

None of atheists' rhetoric and argumentation about "imperfect worlds" disproves anything about God or Christianity. But atheists keep coming back with more fallacious arguments, based on false premises. If we "solve" one problem, they simply come up with another "objection" in their bag of tricks. I've been through the routine myself a hundred times. Many atheists just want to play games when it comes to discussions of Christianity. I've talked to many dozens of them. It's usually not a serious discussion (on occasion it is). They habitually try to "trap" the Christian and make Christianity and Christians look silly (so they can feel better in their self-delusion of atheism and feel mentally superior). That's child's play, not serious thinking or seeking of truth.

Just because Christians may not always have a ready answer to atheists' relentless questioning, that doesn't prove anything. Atheists don't have answers for many things. I have cornered them with logic many times and found that they didn't have an answer. It works both ways. But the bottom line is not to "trap" someone but to share truth with him and get him to see what is false.

The real (*far* more serious) problem is not the problem of evil, but the "problem of good": how does one define "good" without a God? I can attest from long experience in discussion of these matters that the problem of good is exponentially more difficult to resolve than the problem of evil (the most serious and respectable objection to Christianity) ever was or ever will be.

76

Can God Be Blamed for the Nazi Holocaust?

I would say the whole abominable mess of World War II and Hitler could have very easily been prevented if folks had listened to one man: Winston Churchill. But such is the folly of men that they want to believe that everything is fine (the Neville Chamberlain appeasement mentality).

Churchill warned all through the 1930s of the German military buildup, but no one wanted to listen to him. At the same time, Malcolm Muggeridge was exposing Stalin's starving of ten million Ukrainians, but no one wanted to listen to him either.

It's as simple as that. Germany was disarmed after World War I. What happened a mere fifteen years later, when they started building tanks and fighter planes again? Nothing, of course.

C. S. Lewis estimated that four-fifths of the evil in the world is done by man to man. If something as terrible as World War II and the death camps and genocide (and the United States' wiping out of a hundred thousand at a time in Hiroshima, and the dreadful fire bombings of Dresden and Tokyo, so that we aren't innocent either) could have been prevented by the simplest common sense, and listening to one clear-minded man, where do we get off blaming *God* for this idiotic folly of mankind?

Can God Be Blamed for the Nazi Holocaust?

God is no more responsible for abortion than He was for Auschwitz and the other evils in the world. It is brought about by the unchecked evil of men. God wants *us* to do our duty of promoting justice and brotherhood in the world, not to miraculously intervene every time we screw things up yet again.

That part of the problem of evil is very simple to figure out, I think. The hard part is ascertaining why God, knowing how men would act, would allow free will anyway. In that sense, one might try to accuse God of cruelty, but that is where faith and acceptance of what God has revealed, and acknowledgment of our limitations in grasping these very deep mysteries, come in.

Christians see God suffering on the Cross, so we know that He is willing to go through what most of us have to endure: pain, suffering, humiliation, betrayal, et cetera.

People wanted to live in a fantasy world and let the real one go to hell. During World War II, there wasn't a conspiracy against the Jews on the part of all mankind; rather, there was sheer stupidity and ignorance about the man and party who hated Jews and wished to kill them (along with the Slavs, Gypsies, Catholics, handicapped, mentally ill, left-wingers, Protestants, and many other categories, but the Jews were clearly most hated).

The more *primitive* biblical view was that good people prosper and the evil have all kinds of problems. That is true at the very deepest level, and long term, but not short term, and it is seen to be utterly simplistic in terms of this life.

The more developed Old Testament biblical perspective on suffering is that of Job: even the good people suffer (sometimes even extraordinarily, "unfairly" so) and it is ultimately a mystery why, requiring us to trust that God is good and has a purpose, despite all.

That's the whole point of the book of Job (especially the end, where God refers to His omnipotence, omniscience, and providence and says in effect: "Who are you to question anything about me? Where were you when I laid the foundations of the earth?" And so forth.

We must incorporate in our searching for answers, the more advanced, "mysterious" understanding of suffering as seen in Job, Isaiah 53, and many New Testament passages that we Catholics readily apply to the spiritual fruitfulness of penance for the sake of souls (just as prayer and charity do the same good). Suffering has a deep purpose. When we suffer we can apply that to other souls.

We all have to remind ourselves continually that God promises to make things *totally* right only by including the next life in the equation. This world can never be "right" or "normal" because it is a fallen world. All we can do is individually follow God and hope for the best, in temporal terms. We're just pilgrims. But we can have joy and peace despite all. That *is* promised.

Often the problem is that people do not what they should do, in the final analysis, because of "what *others* might think" (peer or social pressure). Half the things I've done in my life (and most of the best, in my opinion) were in the teeth of objections of friends and sometimes, extended family. I would never have become a Catholic or a writer or an apologist. I wouldn't have been in Operation Rescue (a mild form of conscientious protest against an unjust society and mass murder by abortion). I wouldn't have even converted to evangelical Christianity in 1977 (my upbringing was nominal Methodist).

If we're so worried about mere social opinion and what our own circle will think of us, is it any wonder that folks (generally speaking) are so easily cowed into doing the will of dictators and abortion providers, no matter how outrageous, and will endure very little risk in order to avoid speaking out or acting in protest?

Can God Be Blamed for the Nazi Holocaust?

I think what could have been said to those who would have frowned on an early shutdown of Hitler is that there was no particularly compelling reason to think that the man didn't mean to do exactly as he had stated and had written in *Mein Kampf* (one might cite analogous behavior of the Communists who set out and did pretty much what Marx and especially Lenin predicted, and even more).

Hitler was an extremely serious guy. I think anyone could readily see that he meant business. Jews in Germany were certainly well aware of that early on. Why wasn't anyone else? It's the typical latent European anti-Semitism again, I suppose. Combine this with the history of German/Prussian militarism and aggression and the collection of misfits and moral monsters that Hitler was collecting in his government, and it didn't take a rocket scientist to see what was coming. Yet people are quick to blame God for men's follies, imbecilities, blindness, and stupidities.

World War II and all its hideous fruits are squarely the fault of men, not God. It's ridiculous for us to make a royal mess of things and then, when the chickens come home to roost, start whining and moaning, "Why did God allow *this*?" (and then prepare to make the same stupid mistakes all over again; learning absolutely nothing from history).

Indeed, it is an extremely serious and troubling philosophical question: why God allows the human free will that He knew would continually fail and cause great suffering and misery. But that's different from directly blaming God for "doing nothing," during the worst times of our butchering each other.

I think the free will defense in apologetics provides a fairly adequate answer, but there is always a gap left, making it difficult to understand why God allowed a thing that has entailed so much pain and suffering. We can accept it in faith, humbly acknowledging our limitations and God's goodness, but those without faith will understandably struggle quite a bit with it and feel a perplexity that only faith brought about by God's grace and our cooperation with it is ultimately able to overcome.

77

The Inevitability of Development of Doctrine

C. S. Lewis, the famous Anglican apologist, once wrote:

> The positive historical statements made by Christianity have the power ... of receiving, without intrinsic change, the increasing complexity of meaning which increasing knowledge puts into them.

The Catholic Church, in agreement with Lewis, defines doctrinal development as a growth of depth and clarity in the understanding of the truths of divine revelation. It is important to understand that the substantial or essential truths at the core of each doctrine remain unchanged. Only the subjective grasp of men increases.

This increase is the result of the prayerful reflection of the Church, theological study and research (often occasioned by heretical challenges), practical experience, and the collective wisdom of the Church's bishops and popes, especially when joined in ecumenical councils.

Development (often described as an "acorn to oak tree" process) is pictured in the following biblical passage:

Matthew 13:31-32: The kingdom of heaven is like a grain of mustard seed which a man took and sowed in his

Proving the Catholic Faith Is Biblical

field; it is the smallest of all seeds, but when it has grown it is the greatest of shrubs and becomes a tree, so that the birds of the air come and make nests in its branches.

Seeds and bodies grow and expand. Doctrine clearly develops within Scripture (what is also called "progressive revelation"). Examples of this process include the doctrines of the afterlife, the Trinity, the Messiah (eventually revealed as God the Son), the Holy Spirit (a Divine Person in the New Testament), the inclusion of Gentiles, bodily resurrection, and the sacrifice of lambs as a type and shadow of the sacrifice of Christ. Not a single doctrine initially emerges in the Bible complete with no further need of development.

The canon of Scripture itself is an example of developing doctrine (and a Church tradition). The New Testament never informs us which books belong to it, and its list of books took about 360 years to reach its definitive form (at the council of Carthage in A.D. 397).

For instance, the books of Hebrews, James, 2 Peter, 2 and 3 John, Jude, and Revelation were not widely accepted by the Church until 350. Fourteen of twenty-seven New Testament books, including Acts, 2 Corinthians, Galatians, and Colossians, were not mentioned until around A.D. 200.

Today's Church shouldn't be expected to look like the primitive Church if she is a living, vibrant, spiritual organism. But the early Church does already look very "Catholic." What we don't find in the early centuries is a "statue," doomed to be increasingly encroached upon by the "pigeon droppings" of a "corrupting" Catholicism, as is imagined by Protestants of the anti-Catholic variety.

Blessed John Henry Cardinal Newman (1801-1890), in his *Essay on the Development of Christian Doctrine* (1845), the one

The Inevitability of Development of Doctrine

indispensable work on this subject, pointed out that notions of suffering, or "vague forms of the doctrine of Purgatory," were virtually universally accepted in the first four centuries of the Church, whereas, the same cannot be said for the doctrine of Original Sin, which is agreed upon by Protestants and Catholics. Purgatory is not a later corruption, but was present early on and merely developed, and Original Sin was equally subject to development. Cardinal Newman observed:

> If it be true that the principles of the later Church are the same as those of the earlier, then, whatever are the variations of belief between the two periods, the later in reality agrees more than it differs with the earlier, for principles are responsible for doctrines. Hence they who assert that the modern Roman system is the corruption of primitive theology are forced to discover some difference of principle between the one and the other.

This is true whether the theological considerations are those agreed upon by all, such as the divinity of Christ, the two natures of Christ, the Trinity, the Holy Spirit, and Original Sin, or those doctrines denied by all or most Protestants, such as the Marian dogmas, purgatory, the papacy, the Real Presence of Christ in the Eucharist, the Communion of Saints, priestly absolution, baptismal regeneration, and the Sacrifice of the Mass.

One could say that an automobile was "corrupt" if the owner decided that it would run better with half its spark plugs, watered-down gas, no rear brakes, one headlight, and three quarts less oil. Corruption can just as easily consist of subtractions as additions. Protestantism's charges of Catholic corruption, then, only come back to incriminate Protestantism too, since it no longer holds many doctrines that were widely believed in the early Church.

Proving the Catholic Faith Is Biblical

The idea of doctrinal development provides, I believe, the key for understanding why the Catholic Church today often *appears on the surface* as very different from (and contrary to) the early Church.

78

New Testament Proofs of Noah's Existence

Often, Christians act as if the Old Testament is antiquated and of no relevance to Christianity — or, in extreme cases, to history at all. Neither opinion is true. Explaining why would require two long articles; but setting those issues aside, we can still demonstrate how the New Testament regards particulars in the Old Testament. I thought it would be fun, informative, and helpful to apply that "technique" to the question of the historical existence of Noah.

On the Coming Home Network discussion forum that I used to moderate, one of the members related a horror story about a person who was leading a Bible study who taught that Abraham was "the first character in the Bible whom [Catholics] believe actually existed" and that Adam, Eve, Cain, Abel, Noah, and the others "may simply have been literary devices."

This is not Catholic teaching. If Adam and Eve are not regarded as actual persons, and the parents of the human race, then the doctrine of the Fall of Man and Original Sin collapses, and we are not in need of being rescued from a fallen, sinful condition.

The *Catechism* refers to Adam and Eve eight times (nos. 375, 399, 404, 411, 417, 635, 766, 2361), and ties in their rebellion to the Fall of man (nos. 399, 404, 417). St. Paul makes several

Proving the Catholic Faith Is Biblical

historical references to Adam or Eve, or both (Rom. 5:14; 1 Cor. 15:22, 45; 2 Cor. 11:3; 1 Tim. 2:13-14).

Likewise, Cain and Abel are referred to as actual men twice (*Catechism*, nos. 401, 2259), and their actions are also connected to Original Sin. Our Lord Jesus refers quite literally to Abel (Matt. 23:34-35; cf. Luke 11:51). The author of Hebrews includes Abel in his catalogue of the heroes of the faith (Heb. 11:4), and talks about his "blood" (Heb. 12:24).

God made a covenant with Noah. It's pretty difficult to make a covenant with an imaginary, fictional person, and it makes no sense for God to have done that (although it works in Greek mythology). Thus, the *Catechism* refers to Noah and the flood, and what is called the Noachic Covenant, nine times (nos. 56, 58, 71, 701, 845, 1080, 1094, 1219, 2569).

Noah is included in this same recitation of heroic faith, in Hebrews 11. Note how Abraham is mentioned in the next verse. There is no indication whatsoever that one was a real person and the other a mythical figure only:

> **Hebrews 11:7-8**: By faith *Noah*, being warned by God concerning events as yet unseen, took heed and constructed an ark for the saving of his household; by this he condemned the world and became an heir of the righteousness which comes by faith. By faith *Abraham* obeyed when he was called to go out to a place which he was to receive as an inheritance; and he went out, not knowing where he was to go.

St. Peter believed that Noah was a real person too ("God's patience waited in the days of Noah"):

> **1 Peter 3:18-21**: For Christ also died for sins once for all, the righteous for the unrighteous, that he might bring us to God, being put to death in the flesh but made alive in

New Testament Proofs of Noah's Existence

the spirit; in which he went and preached to the spirits in prison, who formerly did not obey, when God's patience waited in the days of *Noah*, during the building of the ark, in which a few, that is, eight persons, were saved through water. Baptism, which corresponds to this, now saves you.

2 Peter 2:4-5, 9: For if God did not spare the angels when they sinned, but cast them into hell and committed them to pits of nether gloom to be kept until the judgment; if he did not spare the ancient world, but preserved *Noah*, a herald of righteousness, with seven other persons, when he brought a flood upon the world of the ungodly ... then the Lord knows how to rescue the godly from trial, and to keep the unrighteous under punishment until the day of judgment.

Again, the text moves from the fallen angels to Noah, and then to Lot (2 Pet. 2:7), who lived in the time of Abraham and was his nephew, to the time he was writing. St. Peter is arguing by analogy, stating, in effect: "God rescued Noah and Lot; He can and will do the same for you today."

This makes absolutely no sense if the earlier people are imaginary, because the text would cite the real fallen angels (demons), then move to the supposedly imaginary Noah, then back to historical reality with Lot and the early Christians. This utterly violates the tenor and nature of the passage, as is the case in similar passages noted above.

I would urge people to stop attending studies "led" by people so uninformed. "Blind guides" lead others astray. It is for very good reason that St. James warns:

James 3:1: Let not many of you become teachers, my brethren, for you know that we who teach shall be judged with greater strictness.

79

Jesus' Use of Socratic Method

I consider myself Socratic in my dialogical method. I almost always go right to the premise and examine it to see if it can hold up. The ancient Greek philosopher Socrates (469-399 B. C.) probably influenced me more than any thinker besides C. S. Lewis, until I was introduced to Blessed John Henry Cardinal Newman's *Essay on the Development of Christian Doctrine* in 1990, which is why my blog has *socrates* in its URL.

I've been mocked on several occasions (especially by certain anti-Catholics) for this love of Socrates and of dialogue. It can hardly be disputed that anyone (Christian or not) who studies philosophy or thinks logically at all is indebted to Socrates—one of the fathers of philosophy.

In a nutshell, the Socratic method is questioning an opponent in dialogue (or sometimes "turning the tables"), to see if what he believes can withstand scrutiny. Jesus and St. Paul did this all the time. Paul frequently disputed and argued with both Jews and Greeks, as the Bible informs us. Jesus questioned His hearers: often the Pharisees or Sadducees, who disbelieved in Him and in various theological or spiritual truths. Here are six examples of Jesus' using this method. Surely many more can be found:

Jesus' Use of Socratic Method

Matthew 6:26-30: Look at the birds of the air: they neither sow nor reap nor gather into barns, and yet your heavenly Father feeds them. Are you not of more value than they? And which of you by being anxious can add one cubit to his span of life? And why are you anxious about clothing? Consider the lilies of the field, how they grow; they neither toil nor spin; yet I tell you, even Solomon in all his glory was not arrayed like one of these. But if God so clothes the grass of the field, which today is alive and tomorrow is thrown into the oven, will he not much more clothe you, O men of little faith?

This is a series of four Socratic-type questions, illustrating the principle of God's provision by analogy. God feeds the birds, and flowers (without working at it) are beautiful, so why worry so much about food and clothing?

Matthew 12:10-11: And behold, there was a man with a withered hand. And they asked him, "Is it lawful to heal on the sabbath?" so that they might accuse him. He said to them, "What man of you, if he has one sheep and it falls into a pit on the sabbath, will not lay hold of it and lift it out?"

In this instance, Jesus asks a Socratic question and makes an accompanying reductio ad absurdum. He shows that the logical consequences of an extreme adherence to the law lead to the absurdity of a sheep being hurt or left to die simply because it is the sabbath day.

Matthew 21:23-27 (esp. 21:24): And when he entered the temple, the chief priests and the elders of the people came up to him as he was teaching, and said, "By what authority are you doing these things, and who gave you this authority?" Jesus answered them, "I also will ask you a question; and if you tell me the answer, then I also will tell you by what authority I do these things. The baptism of John, whence was it? From heaven or from men?" And they argued with one another, "If we say, 'From heaven,' he will say to us, 'Why then did you not believe him?' But if we say, 'From men,' we are afraid of the multitude; for all hold that John was a prophet." So they answered Jesus, "We do not know." And he said to them, "Neither will I tell you by what authority I do these things."

Here, Jesus showed the wrongness of their position through the question that He asked. In truth, John the Baptist was indeed a prophet from God, but they didn't believe this; hence, they couldn't answer His question, which "trapped" them.

Matthew 22:41-45 (esp. 22:42): Now while the Pharisees were gathered together, Jesus asked them a question, saying, "What do you think of the Christ? Whose son is he?" They said to him, "The son of David." He said to them, "How is it then that David, inspired by the Spirit, calls him Lord, saying, 'The Lord said to my Lord, Sit at my right hand, till I put thy enemies under thy feet'? If David thus calls him Lord, how is he his son?"

They reply to the Socratic question and then Jesus logically and theologically "traps" them by explaining the difficulty of their position (Matt. 22:43-45).

Luke 22:67-68: "If you are the Christ, tell us." But he said to them, "If I tell you, you will not believe; and if I ask you [some versions: "a question"], you will not answer."

Jesus' Use of Socratic Method

During His "trial" Jesus is being asked if He is the Messiah (*Christ* in Greek). In usual circumstances, He would, in reply, question His accusers or those who opposed His teachings (using the Socratic method). He implies that here but notes (in His omniscience) that they would not answer any such question from Him anyway.

John 10:31-36: The Jews took up stones again to stone him. Jesus answered them, "I have shown you many good works from the Father; for which of these do you stone me?" The Jews answered him, "It is not for a good work that we stone you but for blasphemy; because you, being a man, make yourself God." Jesus answered them, "Is it not written in your law, 'I said, you are gods'? If he called them gods to whom the word of God came (and scripture cannot be broken), do you say of him whom the Father consecrated and sent into the world, 'You are blaspheming,' because I said, 'I am the Son of God'?"

This is a brilliant series of three Socratic questions, all of which demonstrate the theological bankruptcy and incoherence of the denial of Jesus' divinity.

Another Bible passage also describes the Socratic striving after knowledge (through questioning):

1 Corinthians 8:2: If any one imagines that he knows something, he does not yet know as he ought to know. [Moffatt: Whoever imagines he has attained to some degree of knowledge, does not possess the true knowledge yet.]

The starting point for Socrates was to acknowledge that he did not know (relatively). He said: "What I do not know I do not think I know." If we begin with that premise, we'll always be able to learn more. It's quite possible that St. Paul (being well acquainted with Greek philosophy) had something of the sort in his mind. He's writing to the Corinthians, after all, who were very much cultural Greeks and thus heavily into philosophy.

80

Apologetics Isn't Saying You're Sorry for Your Faith!

It's mostly amusing, but sometimes annoying to be in a field of work that most people have never heard of. "You say you're *sorry* all the time?!" It's good to laugh at yourself.

But seriously, my "job title" originally came from the ancient Greek philosopher Plato and his book *The Apology*, which was about Socrates, another philosopher, vigorously defending himself against false charges of corruption at a trial in Athens (he wound up being sentenced to death).

That was the initial meaning of *apologia*, which is also a biblical word (more on that later). Through common usage it came to mean saying you're sorry. But even today, an effective apology often requires a good *explanation*, which goes back to the root meaning. The Christian (or, more specifically, Catholic) apologist is one who defends Christianity and demonstrates that Christianity is reasonable and credible. In practice, it usually means removing objections or "roadblocks" that trouble or confuse people. We apologists are sort of on the front lines between the Church and the opposing secular culture.

But apologetics is not merely "reactionary" in nature. It's a *positive* endeavor, to bolster the faith of Christians and make them more confident that faith is compatible with reason and solid thinking. We are to love God with our *mind* as well as with all our heart, soul, and strength, as Jesus said (Luke 10:27). If we know *why* we believe *what* we believe, we can more ably and enthusiastically share our Faith with others, as God and the Church call us to do.

The most famous Christian apologist is C. S. Lewis (1898-1963), of *Chronicles of Narnia* and *Shadowlands* (film biography) fame. He was an Anglican professor of English literature, who also wrote apologetics books. Like many of the most influential apologists, he was *not* formally trained in theology. This was also true of G. K. Chesterton (1874-1936), the most beloved and respected Catholic apologist, who was a journalist by trade and never attained a college degree.

Since apologetics is ideally mostly on a "popular" level, I think it's *good* that many who are involved in it are not theologians writing to other scholars (as academics do). The idea is to educate the *masses*. It's more like being a combination of a preacher and a high school teacher (or maybe a private tutor) than being a college professor.

Many apologists are converts from Protestantism. This is good insofar as we converts understand Protestantism from the inside and can therefore more effectively argue against it where we believe it is in error and also point out the significant common ground with our separated brethren.

I'm very grateful for the many good and true things that I learned as an evangelical Protestant. I use them every day — especially the love for Sacred Scripture and the zeal for evangelism that evangelicals are known for. Converts believe that becoming a Catholic is not going from bad to good but, rather, going from very good Christianity to the *fullness* of Christianity.

Apologetics Isn't Saying You're Sorry

Some of the more well-known Catholic apologists today are Scott Hahn, Karl Keating, Patrick Madrid, Jimmy Akin, and Steve Ray. It's a thriving field, with lots of great books, websites, radio shows, and conferences. One might say we are in an age of "apologetics revival."

But unfortunately, many people view apologetics as by nature an arrogant, unsavory, "triumphalistic" activity — putting down others and quarreling endlessly with other Christians and non-Christians. It's not that at all (rightly understood). Yes, we contend for what we think is *most* true, but we can still respect what is true and good in other positions, held in good faith.

We defend positions that we honestly hold and wholeheartedly believe to be true. But at the same time we can *ecumenically* and happily acknowledge the many areas of common ground with other Christians and even other religions, while not compromising our own Catholic beliefs at all. These goals are entirely harmonious.

The classic apologetics Bible passage emphasizes the *spirit* in which we are to engage in it:

1 Peter 3:15: [B]ut in your hearts reverence Christ as Lord. Always be prepared to make a defense [*apologia*] to any one who calls you to account for the hope that is in you, yet do it with gentleness and reverence.

It has to be done in love, with humility, soaked in prayer. The apologist must always keep in mind that it's God who causes a person to become convinced of the Catholic Faith or to become a committed disciple of Christ. It's *all* by God's grace and His power. The apologist is merely a *vessel*. That gets our eyes off ourselves. Any gift or ability that we have comes from God. As we used to say in the evangelical community, "evangelism is one beggar sharing what he has with another beggar."

Another related verse is Jude 3: "[C]ontend for the faith which was once for all delivered to the saints." My favorite of all (what I've always sought to live by, as a model) is St. Paul's self-description:

> **1 Corinthians 9:19, 22-23**: For though I am free from all men, I have made myself a slave to all, that I might win the more.... To the weak I became weak, that I might win the weak. I have become all things to all men, that I might by all means save some. I do it all for the sake of the gospel, that I may share in its blessings.

God saves everyone who is saved, but He chooses to *involve* us in the process. Thus, Paul states that *he* could "save some." Since he often urges us to imitate him, that is our mandate to evangelize and "do apologetics." Obviously, folks have varying levels of ability to do so, and very few specialize in it, by vocation, but we are all called to share our faith in *some* fashion.

About the Author

Dave Armstrong

Dave Armstrong (who was received into the Catholic Church in 1991) has been a full-time Catholic apologist since December 2001. His blog, *Biblical Evidence for Catholicism*, has been online since February 1997, contains over 2,300 papers or web pages, and has been visited by 2.5 million visitors over the last eleven years. Sophia Institute Press has published six of Dave's forty-eight books: *A Biblical Defense of Catholicism* (2003; foreword by Fr. John A. Hardon, S.J.), *The Catholic Verses* (2004), *The One-Minute Apologist* (2007), *Bible Proofs for Catholic Truths* (2009), *The Quotable Newman* (2012), and the present volume. He has been happily married to his wife, Judy, since October 1984; they have three sons and a daughter and reside in southeast Michigan.

An Invitation

Reader, the book that you hold in your hands was published by Sophia Institute Press. Sophia Institute seeks to nurture the spiritual, moral, and cultural life of souls and to spread the Gospel of Christ in conformity with the authentic teachings of the Roman Catholic Church.

Our press fulfills this mission by offering translations, reprints, and new publications that afford readers a rich source of the enduring wisdom of mankind.

We also operate two popular online Catholic resources: CrisisMagazine.com and CatholicExchange.com.

Crisis Magazine provides insightful cultural analysis that arms readers with the arguments necessary for navigating the ideological and theological minefields of the day. *Catholic Exchange* provides world news from a Catholic perspective as well as daily devotionals and articles that will help you to grow in holiness and live a life consistent with the teachings of the Church.

In 2013, Sophia Institute launched Sophia Institute for Teachers to renew and rebuild Catholic culture through service to Catholic education. With the goal of nurturing the spiritual, moral, and cultural life of souls, and an abiding respect for the role and work of teachers, we strive to provide materials and programs that are at once enlightening to the mind and ennobling to the heart; faithful and complete, as well as useful and practical.

www.SophiaInstitute.com
www.CatholicExchange.com
www.CrisisMagazine.com
www.SophiaInstituteforTeachers.org

Sophia Institute Press® is a registered trademark of Sophia Institute. Sophia Institute is a tax-exempt institution as defined by the Internal Revenue Code, Section 501(c)(3). Tax I.D. 22-2548708.